Middle Eastern Delights

60 Delicious, One-of-A-Kind Treats You Need to Try

Lamees AttarBashi

Creator of Cooking with Lamees

PAGE STREET
PUBLISHING CO.

PAGE STREET
PUBLISHING CO.

Copyright © 2024 Lamees AttarBashi
First published in 2024 by
Page Street Publishing Co.
27 Congress Street, Suite 1511
Salem, MA 01970
www.pagestreetpublishing.com

Distributed by Macmillan, sales in Canada by The Canadian Manda Group.

28   27 26   25   24   1 2 3 4 5

ISBN-13: 978-1-64567-924-0
ISBN-10: 1-64567-924-1

Library of Congress Control Number: 2022952209

Cover and book design by Molly Kate Young for Page Street Publishing Co.
Photography by Kara Chin

Printed and bound in the United States

Dedication

To Mothana, Naya and Adam: Thank you for being the best family I could ask for. Thank you for making my days an adventure and my whole life a blessing. I dedicate this book to you!

CONTENTS

Introduction	7	Baklawa Cheesecake	58
About this Book	9	Fig Jam Cold Cheesecake	61
My Arabian Pantry	11	Lazy Cake	62

BAKED GOODIES — 17

Cheese Manakeesh Flatbread	19
Baklawa Pull Apart Bread	20
Churak	23
Maarouk	24
Pistachio Cardamom Rolls	27
Simit	30
Khaliat Al Nahl	33
Kaak Youyou	34

CAKES AND CHEESECAKES — 37

Namoura	39
Kunafa Cheesecake	41
Dates and Walnuts with Salted Caramel Cake	45
Pistachio Cake	46
Almond Cake	49
Baghrir Cake with Rose Infused Frosting	50
Sponge Cake with Pomegranate Glaze	53
Qurs Akili Cake	54
Khanfaroosh	57

BISCUITS, COOKIES AND BITES — 65

Kleicha	67
Maamoul	68
Barazek	71
Kaak Al Asawir	73
Coconut Cookies	77
Ghuraibah	78
Simsimiya	81
Date Balls	82
Baid Al Qata	85

PHYLLO MY HEART — 87

My Mum's Baklawa	89
Almond Briouat	91
Warbat Bil Qishta	95
Asawir Il Sit	96
Zinood Il Sit	99
Phyllo Cigars	102
Muakaja	105
Burma	106
Baklawa Bites	109

KATAIFI DREAMS   111
Kunafa   113
Osmalieh   114
Kunafa Rolls   117

EXTRA SWEET   119
Lukaimat   121
Zlabiya   122
Balah Al Sham   125
Mafrouka   126
Qatayif   129
Stuffed Qatayif   132
Halawat Il Jibn   134
Halwa   137

PUDDINGS AND SOFT DELIGHTS   139
Umm Ali   141
Ishtaliah   142
Leyali Lebnan   145
Tunisian Sabayon   146
Sahlab   149
Roz Bi Haleeb   150
Aish El Saraya   153

ICE CREAMS   155
Simple Booza   157
No-Churn Halwa and Dibis Booza   158
Pistachio Booza   161
Booza Ala Tamur   162

HOT BEVERAGES   164
Chai Aswad   165
Chai Bi Heil   166
Chai Bi Ni'Naa   167
Karak Chai   168
Qahwa   169

Acknowledgments   *170*
About the Author   *172*
Index   *173*

Introduction

This book is about all the recipes that shaped my love affair with desserts and sweets. It all started with my first ever experience inside the kitchen—which was baking a lemon cake after finding the recipe in a kid's book. I was nine at the time and had never laid eyes on a recipe. I ran to my mum and asked her if she could help me make it. My mum—being an amazing cook—was happy to oblige. I remember mixing the sugar with the butter, adding the eggs, then the milk and flour, pouring it into a round metal cake tin and placing it in the oven. The cake needed 45 minutes to fully bake and for that entire time I sat in front of that oven, waiting patiently for it. Needless to say, I ate the whole cake. I was so happy and proud of myself. It was at this exact moment my love for baking and cooking was born.

I grew up in the U.K. as the youngest of four. My father was studying for his master's and doctoral degree at Bradford University in Bradford, West Yorkshire, U.K. There, I was exposed to Middle Eastern food through my mum's cooking and at the same time to British comfort food. One day it was dolma and the next day it was meat pies with Ahh Bisto® gravy. It was always fun coming back home from school, to open the front door and smell what my mom was cooking that day.

From my mom, I started to learn how to cook and realized early on that this was my passion. But in our culture, your choice of career is not based on what your heart desires or where your passion lies, but it's more about what the highest degree your GPA can get you. In my family, you were either a doctor or an engineer—so I got into engineering college. This didn't mean my passion had faded, but I knew that it was never going to be a career path I could choose for myself—just a passion I could practice whenever I had the chance.

Right out of college I got a job in my field, but work became harder to swallow, and with no passion for it, I felt empty inside. Days would go by and the feeling only got worse. Thinking about this period—I remember it all so well—lying on my bed every morning, not wanting to go to work and on one of those mornings, I asked myself, "Imagine yourself five years from now…would you still be feeling this way?" Knowing the answer to my question, I quit my job that same day. I'm no quitter by nature and would fight till the very end, but on that day, I chose happiness and giving myself a chance to work every day on something I was passionate about. It was now or never!

My passion was reignited, and I had a new and deep desire to share my cooking creations with anyone and everyone. I started to chronicle my journey in the kitchen: writing recipes, testing, then taking pictures of the final dish and uploading them on Facebook. I found extreme relief in pouring all my creativity into those recipes. In the beginning, I expected just a few likes and comments, but to my surprise, the posts got way more engagement than I could even imagine. So, I started taking more pictures and posting more, sharing it all with the world. Seeing the response, I decided to take it even further, so I enrolled in culinary arts classes. I was on a roll at this point, cooking and posting on weekdays and attending culinary school on the weekends. My passion and creativity only kept growing, and the numbers online only went higher and higher. I started doing live cooking segments on national TV shows in Dubai and after a few weeks of that, I signed up with the same channel to have my own cooking show *Lamees's Dining Table*. After winning a nationwide cooking competition, things started to have a domino effect. I was offered the opportunity to be a regular on a popular live morning show and be a presenter in nationwide food festivals, which was one of my favorite memories. There's just something about a live audience that no camera can ever replace.

Throughout all of this, there was one thing that I was 100% sure about and that was writing a cookbook. I dreamed about it early on, but never thought it would be possible. I was afraid of my own passion and doubted I'd be able to achieve such a thing. I wrote the table of contents for the book years ago. I wrote at least ten recipes but then just stopped. It felt like it was only a dream at that time, so I kept it on the back burner and didn't take it beyond that point.

In the end, I would like to think that these recipes are like the stories of my childhood and some of my adulthood. Each one carries a memory—memories that I hold dear to my heart, memories that have been formulated either by making, mixing, burning the kitchen down (yep, I did that once!) and lastly tasting each one. I grew up watching my mom cook and bake all the time and now I'm passing on the traditions to my kids and to you!

So, THANK YOU for choosing to buy my first cookbook and I hope you enjoy trying these recipes and making them as much as I do every single time.

From my family to yours,

Lamees

Lamees AttarBashi

About This Book

Sweets are such an iconic and an indispensable part of Arabian cuisine, across all Arab countries. Most people from the Middle East and North African countries have an appetite for all things sugary. These sweets are known for their crunch and fragrance, and they tend to subtly differ in ingredient and/or style from one country to another. In the Arab world, homemade sweets and desserts are gestures of welcome and celebration. A lot of them are considered festive treats that are shared among family as bite-sized desserts, and although each region has its own unique dessert, most use flour, semolina, sugar, butter, eggs, and pistachios or dates which are molded and baked or fried till golden. Even though Arabs lead very busy lives, there's nothing more satisfying for them than making their desserts from scratch. The process itself of making a lot of these celebratory desserts is considered a whole gathering and commemoration. Mums gather their sisters, daughters and sons around a large table where they have already prepped the ingredients, and each person is assigned the task of folding the dessert and placing it in lined sheets ready for the oven. Depending on the amount of ingredients, it can take over an hour or so—but it never felt like a task, since everyone joined in on fun conversations and jokes with a cup of chai or Arabic coffee on the side (and it may or may not have a bite-sized dessert with it). For me, this was my favorite time. These beautiful gatherings and laughter have created the most cherished memories that I hold dear to my heart. I did not know it at that time, but because of these simple tasks of folding and molding a dessert, my hands started memorizing the act and naturally, when I became older and had a house of my own, my hands did not forget and started replicating those motions as if it were yesterday.

MY ARABIAN PANTRY

Growing up, I remember my mother's pantry: filled with spices and herbs and all the delicious condiments she used in her cooking. That pantry was the epitome of her good cooking and successful recipes and I, in turn, learned to create one just the same; carrying my secrets to the flavors to all my recipes. For you to start your journey to create Middle Eastern desserts, there are a few ingredients I would highly recommend you have in your pantry to have ready to go for your creations. Even if you don't recognize them by name, don't be intimidated! Once you get to know them, I promise that they'll enrich your desserts. One of the first things I wanted to explain fully is the pantry section. I feel it's one of the most important sections in the book as it helps readers understand the recipes and how to prepare in advance for them. So here are the most essential items you will need to master the art of making Middle Eastern sweets.

MASTIC

Mastic, also known as *Arabic gum,* is a resin and natural chewing gum obtained from the mastic tree. It is used in a lot of Arabic ice creams, puddings and milk-based desserts. It acts as a thickener and is also used in a lot of Arabic baked goods like Maamoul (page 68).

Taste Profile: Mastic has a very unique pine-like, earthy and somewhat musky flavor. It is the ingredient that gives nabulsi cheese its unique flavor.

Substitution: Vanilla is often used as a substitute instead of mastic. The taste might be a bit different but that is the closest replacement there is. When it is used as a thickener, then use 2 to 3 tablespoons (16 to 24 g) of cornstarch instead of 2 to 3 droplets of mastic (depending on the recipe).

ORANGE BLOSSOM

Orange blossom water is made from the distilled blossoms of orange trees. Flower petals are gently boiled in water, and then aromatic steam is captured and condensed into a catch—producing a clear, fragrant and lightly flavored liquid. It is widely used in Persian, Arabic, Indian and Turkish cuisine, especially desserts as its bitterness cuts through all the sugar nicely.

Taste Profile: Orange blossoms are sweet, citrusy and very potent. A little goes a long way. If you are just starting to introduce it into a recipe, then I would recommend starting with just ½ teaspoon and gradually increasing or decreasing to your liking.

Substitution: An orange blossom water substitute that will retain a punch of citrus is orange extract. Orange extract is very potent, so it is best to add a few drops at a time and then sample.

ROSE WATER

Across the Middle East and North Africa, rose water is used in a lot of the region's sweets and desserts and is often combined with orange blossom. Rose water is produced during the distillation of fresh petals of Damask roses in water until they are highly fragrant. When used accurately, it adds a beautiful floral and fruity background flavor and notes to famous sweets and desserts such as kunafa, Baklawa (page 89), basbousa, mahalabia and so on. The taste is very distinctive and so is its smell—but don't be tempted to go overboard as too much can cause food to taste soapy.

Taste Profile: Much like the flower it comes from, rose water has a floral, sweet, fragrant and delicate quality in its flavor. It has a subtle character to it and needs to be used in moderation to appreciate its true flavor and quality.

Substitution: Vanilla extract is an especially good rose water substitute for baking recipes. You can either choose to use vanilla instead with the same ratio or omit it in its entirety if you are not a fan of its taste. Personally, I make most of my desserts without it as I find its taste too potent, but that's just me.

SEMOLINA

Semolina is a type of flour made from durum wheat. It is very popular in Middle Eastern and North African cuisine. It is found in pasta, couscous and also found in cakes like basbousa, layali, lubnan and used to make the kataifi/kunafa dough (page 113).

Taste Profile: Semolina's taste is not obvious when cooked; however, its earthy aroma is quite distinctive compared to regular wheat flours. Its texture is a bit coarser than traditional flour with a slight golden color to it.

Substitution: Semolina adds a significant texture to the dishes it is used in. However, when substitution is required, all-purpose flour can be used instead. It will not provide you with the rare texture semolina does, but it is the closest one to achieving the same results. Other substitutions might include finely ground cornmeal or corn flour to replicate the texture.

SIMPLE SUGAR SYRUP

This floral simple syrup called *attir* or *atter* is a main component in many Middle Eastern and North African desserts, either by drizzling it on top of the finished product or pouring it directly into it. What makes this syrup different from other sugar syrups is the addition of cardamom, fragrant rose water or orange blossom water. It comes together in less than 15 minutes and lasts for months in your pantry.

*If you like less sugar in your syrup, you can add more water and less time on the stove.

*If your dessert has rose water or orange blossom in its ingredients, it is best to omit it from the sugar syrup to prevent it from overlapping and overshadowing the rest of the ingredients. Personally, I remove them both completely as I like my syrup to have a taste of the cardamom by itself.

QISHTA

Qishta (ishta) is the popular thick cream and crème de la crème of the Arabian cuisine and is used in most of its sweets and desserts. It resembles thick clotted cream in texture but tastes slightly sweeter. It is good by itself, too, with some jam or honey and some fresh warm bread with a cup of warm black tea. Qishta can either be bought from most Middle Eastern stores or can be easily made at home. The one that is made at home tends to be thicker, hence much more suitable in making the desserts in this book and worth the extra 10 minutes to prepare it.

Substitution: Store-bought qishta can be substituted with heavy cream or mascarpone. Replace in a 1:1 ratio.

CARDAMOM

Cardamom is a spindle shaped spice that has an intense taste and aroma to it. It comes in two types: black cardamom and green cardamom, and is used either as a whole pod, as seeds or ground. The green cardamom is what is favored and used in Middle Eastern and North African cuisine.

Taste Profile: Cardamom has a unique slightly spicy, slightly sweet flavor with hints of lemon and mint and is quite aromatic. It is used as a flavor in Arabic cuisine, either ground and added to the desserts—alternatively seeds and pods are either crushed or added whole. The seeds or the whole pod is sometimes added to Arabic coffee and Arabic tea, and it gives them their characteristic flavor. Approximately 12 pods (using seeds only) = 1 teaspoon ground cardamom.

Substitution: The best substitution for ground cardamom are spices that have that same aroma and flavor, such as allspice, cinnamon and nutmeg. Both cinnamon and nutmeg are each widely recommended as cardamom substitutes.

BLACK SEED

Black seed is a tiny black seed that looks like sesame seeds and is sometimes labeled as black caraway or black cumin. It gives a very distinctive flavor profile and fragrance to Middle Eastern baking and pastries, both sweet and savory. It is used to make the very popular cheese—Arabic twisted cheese. It has a mild hint of onion and earthy herbs.

Taste Profile: Black seeds have a slightly bitter taste to them.

Substitution: Although the tastes are quite different, nigella seeds are the closest to black seeds and can be used as a substitute for it.

Usage: It is often used in pastries (both sweet and savory), breads, cheeses and could be ground into a paste and eaten with tahini and honey.

ANISE SEEDS

Anise seeds are called *yansoon* in Arabic. It is a spice native to the Middle East and has a very distinctive aroma, natural sweetness and unmistakable licorice flavor. I remember my mom used to boil them in water and make tea whenever I had stomach aches, and it would always help.

Substitution: Anise seeds look like fennel seeds and have a slightly similar flavor profile, so this would be the best substitution for it. You can also use anise extract. A few drops of it will give you that licorice flavor.

Usage: Anise seed (whole or ground) can be added to the dough for baked goods, fruit fillings for pies and ground meat before baking. It can also be used to flavor drinks such as coffee or hot chocolate or to brew licorice flavored tea.

GHEE

Ghee in Arabic is called *samneh*, and is considered one of the most amazing components in Arabic cuisine as it adds aroma and a very rich flavor—like no other—to any dish. Store bought baklava and kunafa are all made with it. It is also used heavily in savory dishes such as grain dishes, soups and meat stews. Another reason why Arabs love using it is that it doesn't burn as easily as butter as it has a higher smoking point.

Substitution: Although it is not as fragrant as ghee, butter is a great ghee alternative, and it's the most natural ghee substitute because it's formed of the same ingredients as ghee.

MAHLAB/MAHLEB

Mahlab (Mahlebi or *Mayleb)* is an aromatic spice from the *Prunus mahaleb* (mahaleb cherry or St. Lucie cherry). They are light brown in color and resemble small almonds in shape. The seeds are extracted from the cherry pits and ground to a powder. Middle Eastern recipes use the ingredient in cookies, bread, biscuits and ma'moul.

Substitution: If you cannot find mahlab spice, you can substitute it with a ratio of 2:1 with ground cinnamon and caraway seeds. Another substitution would be a combination of almond extract and star anise.

Taste Profile: When mahlab hits your tongue, it will taste a bit like a cherry, a bit like almond with a hint of vanilla (similar to marzipan), with a subtle anise undertone and an aftertaste of bitterness. When cooked—everything changes. It becomes fruity and rich, but very subtle. It's like one of those spices that elevates your dish to a whole other level.

SAHLEP POWDER

Sahlep (salep) is a flour made from the bulbs of the wild orchid genus *Orchis*. It is a popular ingredient in the Middle East and is used in ice cream, beverages and many desserts.

Substitution: Since sahlep is a thickening agent, it can be substituted with cornstarch to mimic the thick texture.

Baked Goodies

Baking is probably my favorite way of making sweets. There is something about the process of making them that is so satisfying and therapeutic to me. I only recently bought a stand mixer. Before that, I would do most of the process of kneading by hand—just the way I saw my mum do it. But now with two kids, two businesses and a house to run, I had to find shortcuts to quickly make the recipes that I love the most. Don't get me wrong, I miss the feeling of pushing the dough and kneading it with my knuckles *tremendously*, but I've come to appreciate the technology that we have today and how it has made our lives a tad easier.

In this chapter, you will find a lot that will spark your curiosity—a tantalizing array of baked goodies, from the beautiful braided Churak (page 23) to the soft and nutty Baklawa Pull Apart Bread (page 20) to the famous Cheese Manakeesh Flatbread (page 19) and so much more. Grab a cup of black tea and enjoy the doughy ride.

Cheese Manakeesh Flatbread

Manakeesh, or in singular form man'ousheh, *is a Lebanese street food—a very popular breakfast that is eaten on the go and very similar to a pizza. The dough is very soft and is usually topped with a variety of options. The first time I ever tasted manakeesh was when I was 28 years old working as a program manager. My working buddy, who was Palestinian, invited me to try it over breakfast. The bakery was only 5 minutes away from the office, so we decided to walk there and once we arrived, we entered the small bakery that was situated in a tiny alley behind major buildings. As soon as I was close to the entrance, I could smell the beautiful and delicious aroma of freshly baked goods with a hint of cheese and the distinctive smell of za'atar. There I was presented with 3 options: za'atar manakeesh, cheese manakeesh and labna with vegetables manakeesh. I was mesmerized by the gooeyness of the melted cheese, so I opted for that one, which was made in 5 minutes or less. As soon as it comes out of the oven, it gets folded in half and wrapped with parchment paper and handed directly to you. I still, to this day, fondly remember that smell and aroma and the whole experience and luckily for me—it is extremely easy to make at home.*

Yield 7 Pieces

For the Cheese Topping

4 cups (500 g) white cheese or mozzarella, grated

1½ cups (200 g) feta cheese, crumbled

¼ cup (56 ml) olive oil

For the Dough

2 tsp (6 g) active dry yeast

1 tsp granulated sugar

1 cup (240 ml) water, lukewarm (110°F [43°C]), divided

3¼ cups (400 g) all-purpose flour

2 tbsp (20 g) powdered milk

½ tsp salt

3 tbsp (42 g) olive oil

Black seeds or Nigella seeds, for garnish

Note *Manakeesh can be placed in a zip tight bag and into the refrigerator for 2-3 days. Just take it out before serving and preheat it either in a microwave or in the oven for an extra crisp.*

To make the cheese mixture, add the mozzarella and feta cheese with the olive oil to a large bowl and rub the mixture well with your fingers until well combined. Cover with plastic wrap and set aside.

To make the dough, start by combining yeast, sugar and ⅓ cup (80 ml) of the warm water in a small bowl. Whisk until yeast and sugar have completely dissolved. Leave to proof for 10 minutes.

To prepare the dough, sift flour into a stand mixer bowl. Add powdered milk, salt and the yeast mixture into the bowl (once it has been proofed). Add the oil and the ⅔ cup (160 ml) remaining of the warm water. Knead for 4 to 5 minutes until a nice consistent dough is formed. Drizzle a bit of olive oil in the empty mixing bowl to prevent it from sticking, and place the dough back in. Cover with plastic wrap and a large towel to keep it warm and help it rise faster. Place it in the warmest area in the kitchen and let it rest for at least 2 hours.

Place a rack in the middle of the oven and preheat to 375°F (190°C). Line two large baking sheets with parchment paper and spray with oil. Lightly flour your work surface and turn the dough in. Divide the dough into seven equal balls, which should usually weigh 3½ ounces (100 g) each. Cover the dough balls with a kitchen towel and let them rest for another 20 minutes. Work with one ball at a time and cover the rest. Roll each dough ball into a 6 to 8-inch (15 to 20-cm) circle and transfer it onto one of the baking sheets. Top each circle with 3½ ounces (100 g) of the cheese mixture and 1 to 2 teaspoons (5 to 10 g) of black seeds. Bake for 10 minutes then broil for 2 minutes until golden and crispy. Take them out and serve with a cup of Chai Aswad (page 165).

Baklawa Pull Apart Bread

This nutty goodness is taking baklawa to a whole other level. Imagine the nutty mixture of a baklawa but with the softness of a bread. That is precisely what this is—layers upon layers of soft, fluffy and delicate bread with a thin layer of a sugary nut mixture in between, topped with a drizzle of simple sugar syrup. So, if you love baklawa and bread then you will love this one too!

Yield 6–8 Servings

For the Dough

3½ tbsp (50 ml) water, lukewarm (110°F [43°C])

2 tsp (7 g) active dry yeast

⅓ cup (63 g) granulated sugar, divided

¼ cup (55 g) unsalted butter

⅔ cup (160 ml) whole milk

2 large eggs

4⅔ cups (575 g) all-purpose flour

1 tsp vanilla extract

For the Filling

¼ cup (60 g) unsalted butter, melted

½ cup (100 g) granulated sugar

¾ cup (100 g) raw unsalted pistachios, chopped

½ cup (55 g) walnuts, chopped

2 tsp (6 g) ground cinnamon

½ tsp salt

For the Simple Sugar Syrup

½ cup (100 g) granulated sugar

1 cup (240 ml) water

2 cardamom pods

For Garnishing

1 egg, whisked for brushing

Pistachios, chopped

To prepare the dough, in a small bowl add the water, yeast and 1 tablespoon (15 g) of sugar and mix well until fully dissolved. Let it proof for 10 minutes. In a large saucepan, warm butter, milk and the remaining sugar on low heat. As soon as the butter melts and the sugar is fully dissolved, remove from the heat and transfer to a stand mixer bowl. Let it cool down slightly before adding in the eggs, then add the flour, vanilla extract and the yeast mixture. With the dough attachment, mix well on medium speed until the ingredients start to form a soft dough, around 4 to 5 minutes. Transfer to a bowl lightly greased with oil, cover with plastic wrap and a kitchen towel. Let it rest and rise to double the volume for at least 2 hours.

To prepare the filling, add butter, sugar, pistachios, walnuts, cinnamon and salt to a medium-sized bowl. Mix well then set aside.

Dust a working bench with flour and roll out the dough using a rolling pin until the thickness is about ¼ inch (½ cm)—no less or it will be hard to carry it to the pan. Roll it out until the size is around 18 x 15-inches (45 x 38-cm). Take a large spatula and spread the filling evenly on the entire dough. With a knife, slice it into 14 to 15 square pieces. Place the first five on top of each other and transfer to a greased 9 x 4-inch (22 x 10-cm) bread pan. Repeat the process until all the dough squares are in the pan (don't worry if there is still space in the pan, the dough will expand further and fill it up). Cover the pan with greased plastic wrap and let it rest for 2 hours.

Preheat the oven to 350°F (180°C). Brush it with egg wash and bake the bread for 35 to 40 minutes or until golden. After 30 minutes, if necessary, lay a piece of aluminium foil on top of the bread to prevent top of bread from burning.

To prepare the sugar syrup, add sugar, water and cardamom to a small saucepan and whisk until the sugar is dissolved. Boil on medium heat for 15 minutes, or until it slightly thickens and reduces by ⅓. Remove from the heat and let it cool.

Take the bread out of the oven and drizzle with sugar syrup while it is still hot. Let the bread cool for 10 minutes before removing it from the pan. Garnish with pistachios and serve warm with a cup of Chai Aswad (page 165) or Qahwa (page 169).

Churak

My mum loved baking for us when we were kids, and one of her favorite things to make was churak. They were extremely soft, airy and a pleasant treat. The batches she made were not merely small ones but rather massive ones. I would watch her make them for hours and would chime in when it was time to braid them—this is the real reason why I'm so good at braiding now. After they were fully baked, she would place them in a ziplock bag and in the freezer where they would be enjoyed for months. My mum had three freezers, so storage was never an issue. She did, however, try to hide those bags deep in those three freezers in hopes we didn't eat it all and keep some for our guests when they would visit. I would try my best not to go find them but alas, I could never resist and dived into those freezers to find them—which took me less than 10 minutes. I took one out and enjoyed consuming the delicious churak without being detected and then did the same thing the next day ... let's just say she was quite surprised how little remained when she took the bag out for one of our guests. Sorry mum but I have no regrets here! Those soft, airy churak were so addictive, especially served with a cup of milk mixed with 1 tablespoon (4.5 g) of Nescafé® coffee granules. I would dip and eat it like there was no tomorrow!

Yield 8 Servings

For the Dough

½ cup (120 ml) water, lukewarm (110°F [43°C])

1 tbsp (10 g) active dry yeast

1 cup (200 g) and 1 tbsp (15 g) granulated sugar, divided

1 cup (240 ml) whole milk, lukewarm (110°F [43°C])

2 eggs, room temperature

½ cup (113 g) butter, melted

1 tsp vanilla extract

1 tsp salt

7 cups (875 g) all-purpose flour

For the Egg Wash

1 egg

1 tsp vanilla extract

½ tsp white vinegar

For Garnishing

Sesame seeds (optional)

To prepare the dough, in a stand mixing bowl, add the warm water, yeast and 1 tablespoon (15g) sugar. Whisk well until fully dissolved and let it proof for up to 10 minutes. Add milk, 1 cup (200g) of sugar, eggs, butter, vanilla extract and salt and whisk until fully combined, around 15 seconds. Using a dough attachment, start adding the flour gradually and continue mixing on low to medium speed for up to 5 minutes until the dough has been formed. Cover with plastic wrap and a large towel and let it rest for at least 2 hours or until it doubles in size.

Preheat oven to 350°F (180°C). Prepare a baking sheet with parchment paper and sprinkle flour on a working bench. Place the dough on top, knead gently and start forming a 4 x 12-inch (10 x 30-cm) cylinder. With a sharp knife, cut 1-inch (2.5-cm) slices then roll until it forms into a thin string with an approximate length of 6 to 8 inches (15 to 20 cm). Take one piece, while making sure the rest are covered with a towel to prevent them from drying out, then tie the piece into a knot and wrap the ends inwards to form a circular shape, like a pretzel. You can also shape the dough into a braid using 3 strings and tuck the 2 ends underneath firmly to prevent it from opening when baking. Place it on the baking sheet, repeat the process, cover and let it rest for 10 minutes. Whisk the egg with the vanilla and vinegar then brush each piece gently, making sure you do not press too hard and damage the shape.

Sprinkle with sesame seeds if you want, then place them in the oven for 15 to 20 minutes then broil for 3 minutes or until golden. Take them out and serve with Qahwa (page 169) or Chai Aswad (page 165).

Maarouk

This is one of my favorite Syrian brioche-like breads that bring back fond memories every time I make them. They are sweet and soft with a delicious aroma of cardamom, anise and mahlab. Stuffed with dates, sprinkled with sesame seeds and sometimes black nigella seeds for an extra layer of flavor, then finally brushed with simple sugar syrup as soon as they are out of the oven to give it that shiny glaze. They can be shaped in many ways like a braid, spiral or a twist but the most popular way is a cylindrical bracelet with several slits on the side. Maarouks are good for an afternoon snack with a warm beverage like tea or coffee.

Yield 11–13 Pieces

For the Date Filling

16–17½ oz (450–500 g) medjool dates, pitted

3 tbsp (45 g) unsalted butter, melted

1 tsp ground cardamom

For the Dough

1 cup (240 ml) whole milk, lukewarm (110°F [43°C])

2 tsp (7 g) active dry yeast

½ cup (100g) granulated sugar

2 large eggs

⅓ cup (75 g) unsalted butter, melted

1 tbsp (15 ml) white vinegar

4¾ cups (600 g) all-purpose flour

1 tsp mahlab powder (optional)

1 tsp ground anise

1 tsp baking powder

2 tbsp (15 g) powdered milk

1 tsp salt

To make the date filling, add all the ingredients to a pan, using a spatula to soften up the dates. Cook on low to medium heat for about 6 to 8 minutes until a smooth paste has formed. Transfer to a bowl, cover with plastic wrap and set aside to cool.

To make the dough, add warm milk, yeast and sugar to a stand mixer bowl and whisk well using a whisk attachment to activate the yeast. Let it proof for 10 minutes then add the eggs, melted butter and vinegar and mix well until fully combined. In a separate bowl, mix the flour with the mahlab (if using), ground anise, baking powder, milk powder and salt. Switch to the dough attachment then gradually add the flour mixture to the wet ingredients. Start kneading slowly then increase to medium speed once all the flour mixture has been combined with the wet mixture. Keep kneading for about 5 minutes until you have a smooth and elastic dough. The dough should be smooth, so if it feels a bit sticky, add another ¼–⅓ cup (30–50 g) of flour and knead for another 5 minutes. Remove the dough from the bowl, add a bit of oil and place the dough back in. Cover with plastic wrap and a towel and leave to rest in a warm place for 2 to 3 hours or until the dough has doubled in size.

To make the rings, using a rolling pin, roll out a 3-ounce (80-g) piece of dough until you have a 6 x 8-inch (15 x 20-cm) rectangular shape with a ⅓ inch (8 mm) thickness. Roll out a 1–1½ inch (2.5-4 cm) piece of the date filling so you have a rope shape that is 8 inches (20 cm) long and less than ½ inch (1.25 cm) thick. Place that date rope onto the long side of the dough and gently roll the dough starting from the date filling toward the other side. Roll it around three times, cut any excess dough and roll it back and forth to create an even shaped string then bring the two ends of the dough together to create a ring shape and pinch the sides to seal them. Using a knife, make cuts all around the ring with at least ½ inch (1.25 cm) space between and about five to eight cuts. Transfer to an oven sheet with double parchment paper. Let it rest for 10 to 15 minutes, covered. In the meantime, preheat the oven to 380°F (195°C).

(continued)

Maarouk (continued)

For the Egg Wash

1 egg yolk

½ tsp instant coffee

¼ tsp vegetable oil

For Garnishing

Sesame seeds

Black seeds or Nigella seeds

For the Sugar Syrup

¼ cup (50 g) granulated sugar

½ cup (120 ml) water

Prepare the egg wash by whisking the egg, instant coffee and vegetable oil together in a small bowl. Then brush the top of each maarouk, sprinkle on sesame seeds and black seeds and bake for 16 to 18 minutes. Then, broil on low for an additional 2 to 3 minutes until golden.

To make the sugar syrup, mix all the sugar and water in a small saucepan, and bring to a boil on medium heat. Let it boil for 5 minutes, then remove from the heat and let it cool down completely. Once the maarouk bread is done, brush a bit of the sugar syrup on top of each piece. Serve with Chai Aswad (page 165) or Qahwa (page 169).

Notes

- *If some of the maarouk do not hold their shape after pinching the ends, you can brush a bit of the egg wash mixture on the edges just before sealing them.*

- *To make sure the maarouk does not over bake from the bottom, try adding another baking sheet below the one with the maarouk.*

- *Maarouk can be kept in an airtight bag in the fridge for up to 10 days.*

- *If the dough has been rolled out three times when making the ring shape, then keep in mind it will need an additional 2 minutes in the oven.*

Pistachio Cardamom Rolls

These sweet and fluffy pistachio cardamom rolls with a rose water glaze have been a family favorite for a while now. They are light, buttery brioche-like dough that is smothered with a delicious rose water glaze on top. The pistachio paste has an array of flavors and aromas including rose water, cardamom and cinnamon that gives it a lovely depth of flavor. Sometimes I like to eat it on its own without the glaze, when I am craving less sugar and more dough; but however you choose to eat it, it will be a really enjoyable experience.

Yield 8 Rolls

For the Pistachio Paste

1¼ cups (150 g) raw unsalted pistachios

⅔ cup (80 g) powdered sugar

½ tsp salt

1 tsp cardamom (optional)

1 tsp cinnamon (optional)

3 tbsp (45 g) ghee or butter, softened

1 tsp rose water (optional)

1 tbsp (15 ml) water

For the Dough

⅔ cup (160 ml) whole milk, lukewarm (110°F [43°C])

2 tsp (7 g) active dry yeast

2 tbsp (25 g) granulated sugar

2 medium-sized eggs

¼ cup (60 g) unsalted butter, softened

1 tsp vanilla extract

3½ cups (440 g) all-purpose flour

To make the pistachio paste, start by blanching the pistachios in boiling water for 3 minutes to remove the skin. Then transfer them to a bowl with cold water and leave them for 2 to 4 minutes. Next, peel the skin with your fingers while they are still in the cold water. Then place them on a clean towel to dry and once they are dry, add the pistachios to a food processor. Process for 6 to 8 minutes until the paste starts to form. (You might need to scrape it down a couple of times). Add the powdered sugar, salt, cardamom, cinnamon and process for 5 minutes. While still processing, add the butter, rose water (if you are choosing to use) and water. Continue to process until it's very smooth and has the consistency of a nutty paste. Scoop the paste into a bowl and set aside.

To make the dough, add the warm milk, yeast and sugar to a small bowl and whisk well until fully dissolved. Let it proof for 10 minutes. In a stand mixer bowl, add eggs, butter, vanilla extract and yeast mixture and mix until fully combined. Then start gradually adding the flour while mixing slowly and with a dough attachment. Knead for 5 to 6 minutes on medium speed until a smooth dough starts to form. Cover with plastic wrap and a towel and let it rest for 2 hours or until the dough has doubled in volume.

Sprinkle flour on a working bench and roll out the dough into a 12 x 16-inch (30 x 45-cm) rectangular shape. Spread the pistachio paste evenly, covering the dough entirely, leaving at least ½ inch (1.25 cm) space on one side of the dough. Brush that edge with a bit of water and start rolling the dough from the filled edge towards the empty edge until you have a log-shaped roll. Either using a thin string–like unscented dental floss or a serrated knife for clean and smooth cuts, cut the log into eight equal pieces. Then place them on their side in a greased 10–inch (25–cm) cast iron pan. Cover the pan loosely with plastic wrap and a kitchen towel and let rise for up to 1 hour. While the rolls are resting, preheat the oven to 350°F (180°C).

Place the pan in the oven and bake for 25 minutes.

(continued)

Pistachio Cardamom Rolls (continued)

For the Rose Water Cream

2¼ cups (260 g) powdered sugar

5 tbsp (75 ml) heavy cream

1 tsp rose water

To make the rose water cream, place the sugar and cream in a stand mixer with a whisk attachment and whisk for 6 to 8 minutes or until creamy and smooth. Add the rose water at the last minute. Spread the rose cream on top of the buns while still warm and serve with Karak Chai (page 168) or Chai Aswad (page 165).

Simit

Iraqi simit is a delicious sesame crusted circular bread that is dunked in molasses and encrusted with sesame seeds. Originally from Türkiye, it spread throughout the Middle East during the Ottoman Empire. Iraqi simit is slightly thinner compared to the Turkish one. I remember driving with my family through the streets of Baghdad and would encounter a street vendor with a tray full of simit bracelets balanced on his head at nearly every traffic light, moving around the cars shouting "Sameet . . . Sameet!". I was simply mesmerized by those street vendors and their ability to walk with that huge tray on their head with NO HANDS holding it up, so I would always buy one or two. They are crunchy and slightly chewy with a nutty taste that comes from the toasted sesame sprinkled on all sides.

Yield 10 Servings

For the Dough

2 tsp (7 g) active dry yeast

¼ cup (50 g) granulated sugar, divided

1 cup (240 ml) water, lukewarm (110°F [43°C]), divided

6¾ cups (850 g) all-purpose flour, sifted

1 tsp kosher salt

3½ tbsp (50 ml) vegetable oil

1 cup (240 ml) whole milk, room temperature

For the Liquid Dip

¼ cup (70 ml) date molasses

2 tbsp (30 ml) water

1 tsp flour

For Garnishing

½ cup (70 g) sesame seeds

Note *To store leftovers in the freezer, once cooled down, place them in an airtight bag and freeze for up to 6 months. Take out and let it thaw for 10 minutes before baking it for 10 minutes in the oven on 300°F (160°C).*

To make the dough, place active yeast, 2 tablespoons (25 g) of sugar and 3½ tablespoons (50 ml) of water in a small bowl. Whisk until all yeast grains have dissolved and leave to proof for 10 minutes. In a stand mixer bowl, using the dough attachment, add flour, yeast mixture, salt, the remaining sugar and oil and mix for one minute. Add the milk and the remaining water and mix for 6 to 8 minutes or until it forms into a dough, and it is not sticky. Cover with plastic wrap and a towel and let the dough rise in a warm section of the kitchen for 2 hours or until it doubles in size.

To make the liquid dip, mix the molasses, water and flour and set aside. Toast the sesame seeds in a pan for 3 minutes on low heat, making sure you don't overly toast it as it will continue toasting with the simit in the oven later. Place the toasted sesame seeds in a bowl and set aside.

Take the dough out from the mixing bowl and place it on a floured working bench. Divide the dough into 20 equal pieces approximately 2½ ounces (70 g) each. Take two and cover the rest with a towel. Roll the two pieces into a rope around 20–25 inches (50-64 cm) in length and 1 inch (2.5 cm) in thickness and lay them parallel to each other. Begin to roll in the opposite directions to form a twist or a braid, hold the ends and pinch them together to seal, forming a ring. Let it rest on an oven sheet with parchment paper. Repeat the process until you have ten pieces on two trays. Cover and let them rest for another 30 minutes, while you preheat the oven to 380°F (194°C).

After the 30 minutes, dip them completely into the molasses mixture and dunk in the sesame seeds until covered on all sides. Bake for 18 to 22 minutes or until golden. Take them out and place on a cooling rack and serve with Chai Aswad (page 165).

Khaliat Al Nahl

Honeycomb bread is a popular treat in many Arab countries such as Iraq, Lebanon and Yemen. Khaliat al nahl translates to bee honeycomb, due to the resemblance in appearance. The balls are fluffy and soft in texture, and glazed with sweet honey, making it one of my favorites as a kid. What I love about it the most is the variety of ways to make it—you can make it plain or stuff it with cream or cheese. Honeycomb balls are great as an appetizer, a snack or a light dinner.

Yield 15 Balls

For the Dough

1 egg

1 cup (240 ml) whole milk, lukewarm (110°F [43°C])

¼ cup (60 g) butter, melted

2 tbsp (30 g) sugar

1 tsp baking powder

1 tbsp (10 g) active dry yeast

1 tsp salt

3¾ cups (460 g) all-purpose flour

1 cup (225 g) cream cheese

For the Egg Wash

1 egg

1 tbsp (15 ml) milk

1 tsp vanilla extract

For Garnishing

Handful sesame seeds

Handful black or Nigella seeds

2-3 tbsp (30-45 ml) honey

In a stand mixer bowl, and using a wire whip attachment, whisk the egg, warm milk and melted butter. Add the sugar, baking powder, yeast, salt and continue to whisk for 1 more minute. Change the attachment to the dough hook and start adding 1 cup (125 g) of flour at a time while mixing. Continue kneading until your dough is soft and not sticky, around 5-6 minutes. Let your dough rest, covered loosely with plastic wrap and a kitchen towel for 2 hours until it doubles in size. On a floured surface, shape the dough into fifteen balls and place them on a greased baking sheet. Cover and let rest for 30 minutes.

Flatten each ball using a rolling pin and place 1 tablespoon (15 g) of cream cheese in the center of each ball of dough. You can put around 2 tablespoons (30 g) of cheese if you prefer it to have more cheese stuffing. Wrap the dough around the cheese and seal well. Then place the balls in a 10-inch (25-cm) greased cast iron pan. Cover the pan and let your dough rest until the balls rise, around 30 minutes or until they double in size.

Preheat your oven to 380°F (195°C).

In a small bowl, mix the egg, milk and vanilla extract to prepare the egg wash and whisk until well combined. Then brush the balls with the egg wash and sprinkle some sesame seeds and black seeds on top. Bake for 18 to 20 minutes on the middle rack then broil for 1 to 2 minutes until golden. Brush honey on the honeycomb bread while it's still warm. Serve warm with Chai Aswad (page 165).

Kaak Youyou

Kaa'k yoyo (also referred to as youyou) is a traditional Tunisian sweet that looks like a donut but is dunked in sugar syrup or honey instead of the usual powdered sugar. They are sweet, fragrant, fluffy and traditionally eaten with coffee or mint tea with pine nuts in the afternoon.

Yield 8 Donuts

For the Simple Syrup

1 cup (240 ml) water

2 cups (400 g) of granulated sugar

2 cardamom pods

½ lemon, juiced

1 tbsp (15 ml) orange blossom water (optional)

For the Dough

3 eggs

3½ tbsp (50 ml) olive oil

¼ cup (50 g) granulated sugar

3 tbsp (45 ml) milk

1 tbsp (15 ml) orange blossom water

2 tsp (9 g) baking powder

Pinch of salt

3⅓ cups (415 g) all-purpose flour

6-8 cups (1.4-1.8L) vegetable oil

For Garnishing

⅔ cup (75 g) raw pistachios, chopped

Handful of rose petals

To prepare the simple syrup, pour water, sugar and cardamom in a medium-sized saucepan. Bring to a boil then add the lemon juice and orange blossom water (if using). Simmer on medium heat for about 15 minutes until the syrup has thickened slightly. Set the syrup aside to cool down.

To prepare the dough, in a stand mixer bowl, add the eggs, oil, sugar, milk and orange blossom water. Mix for 1 minute until homogeneous. In a separate bowl, mix the baking powder, salt and the flour then pour gradually into the liquid mixture while constantly whisking on low speed until the dough has formed and is slightly sticky. Cover with plastic wrap and a large towel and let rest at room temperature for 1 hour.

Prepare a working bench by sprinkling flour on top and begin to roll out the dough using a rolling pin. Continue to roll until the dough is ⅓ inch (8 mm) thick. Using a round cookie cutter, cut the dough into circular shapes. Then with a smaller round cookie cutter or your knife, cut a ½-inch (1.25-cm) circle right in the middle of each larger circle to get that donut look. Let it rest covered for another 20 minutes.

Add the vegetable oil to a large deep pot over medium heat and once the temperature reaches 375°F (190°C), add the youyous 3 to 4 at a time. Deep-fry for up to 1½ minutes on each side or until golden. Drain on a plate lined with paper towel, then dip the youyous into the sugar syrup and turn them over so that they are well coated. Drain to remove the excess syrup before placing them on a serving tray. Sprinkle with pistachios and rose petals. Serve with Moroccan tea or Qahwa (page 169).

Note *Youyous can be kept in an airtight container at room temperature for up to 2 days and in the fridge for up to 5 days.*

Cakes and Cheesecakes

My very first experience in the kitchen was baking a lemon cake, and as much as I enjoyed eating it alone when I was 9–I believe cakes are very festive and are best shared with the people you love. This applies to cheesecakes too! And when you add a bit of Arabian flair, you transform them to a star centerpiece for your table and a true crowd pleaser amongst your family and friends, like the Baklawa Cheesecake (page 58) and the Kunafa Cheesecake (page 41). They are true representations of when East meets West.

Namoura

Namoura is an extremely moist, buttery flavored and melt in your mouth kind of dessert which first originated in Egypt. Since then, it has spread widely to the rest of the Middle Eastern and Mediterranean countries. A lot of those countries have developed their very own version of making it under different names like harissa *and* basbousa *to name a few. Variations include additional ingredients like coconut, ghee (instead of butter) and a thick cream stuffing.*

Yield 10 Servings

For the Sugar Syrup

½ cup (100 g) granulated sugar

2-3 cardamom pods, cracked

½ cup (120 ml) water

½ lemon, juiced

For the Namoura

2 cups (350 g) course semolina

¾ cup (75 g) shredded coconut

1 tsp baking powder

½ cup (100 g) granulated sugar

1 egg

½ cup (120 ml) vegetable oil

½ cup + 2 tbsp (150 ml) whole milk

½ cup (165 ml) Greek yogurt

1 tsp vanilla extract

For the sugar syrup, add the sugar, cardamom pods and water to a medium-sized saucepan and place it on the stove over medium heat. Let it boil for 8 to 10 minutes until all the sugar has dissolved. Then add the lemon juice before setting it aside to cool completely. Cooling normally takes around 20 minutes.

To prepare the namoura, mix the semolina, coconut, baking powder and sugar together in a large bowl until well combined. In a separate bowl, beat the egg for 30 seconds then add the oil, milk, yogurt and vanilla. Whisk together for 2 minutes on low speed until the texture becomes creamy and smooth. Then pour the wet mixture over the dry mixture. Using a spatula, gently mix until all ingredients are fully combined. (Just make sure you do not over mix it as it might start to separate). Preheat the oven to 350°F (180°C). Spray a 10-inch (25-cm) round tart pan with oil and pour all the mixture in and spread evenly. Now you might notice the surface is a bit bumpy. This can easily be solved by pouring 1 tablespoon (15 ml) of any oil on top of the namoura and patting the oil gently all over using the back of the spoon until it is completely smooth.

(continued)

Namoura (continued)

For Garnishing

½ cup (72 g) blanched almonds, cut in half lengthwise

Thick whipped cream or vanilla ice cream

Because namoura is a very delicate dessert, we have to cut it two times before it is fully baked; one time is before we place it in the oven, and the second time is when it's halfway through baking. If you try to cut it after baking, it will only crumble and will not have beautiful defined shapes to it. With a sharp knife, cut through vertically and diagonally to create diamond shaped pieces and then place half a blanched almond gently on top of each of those diamonds. Place the pan in the middle rack of the oven for 20 minutes. Then, take it out and gently cut the diamonds again and place it back in the oven and continue baking for another 20 minutes or until golden. Let it rest and cool for 5 minutes before pouring the sugar syrup (which should be at room temperature) evenly on top of the pan. Let it cool for an hour before serving it with thick whipped cream or vanilla ice cream.

Notes

- *You can stuff the namoura with thick cream or qishta (page 14) by layering half the mixture in the pan, baking it for 25 minutes then adding 2 cups (450 g) of qishta on top. Lastly, cover it with the remaining half of the mixture and bake it for 25 minutes. It might need an extra 5 minutes to fully bake.*

- *You can also add 1 tablespoon (15 ml) of cold qishta on the top of each piece of namoura. It will provide a smooth and creamy finish to every bite.*

- *To blanch almonds, place raw almonds in a pot, cover with water and let boil for 20 to 25 minutes on medium heat. Drain the almonds and then run under tap water. Peel the almonds easily by squeezing them out of the skin.*

- *In Middle Eastern sweets that require pouring simple sugar syrup on top, it is vital that one of them (the dessert or the syrup) must be room temperature (preferably the syrup) to avoid the dessert from becoming soggy and overly sweet and to maintain its crunchiness.*

Kunafa Cheesecake

This cheesecake is made of sweet and crunchy golden kataifi *dough with sweet cream cheese sandwiched in between. It's where East meets West to make one of the best desserts you could taste. This recipe is a decadent version of Middle Eastern inspired cheesecake. It is creamy and rich with a drizzle of sugar syrup.*

Yield 10–12 Servings

For the Cheesecake

4 cups (950 g) cream cheese

1 cup (200 g) granulated sugar

½ cup (120 ml) heavy cream

1 tsp vanilla extract

5 eggs

Preheat oven to 325°F (165°C).

Prepare a 9-inch (22-cm) cake pan by spraying the inside with oil and lining the bottom and sides with parchment paper then spraying again. Wrap the outside of the pan with aluminum foil, covering the bottom and sides of the pan to prevent any water from leaking into the cheesecake. Find a larger baking dish that will accommodate your cake pan inside comfortably and allow you to fill the baking dish with water, and set to the side.

To prepare the cheesecake, place the cream cheese in a stand mixer bowl and beat until creamy for around 2 to 3 minutes. Then add the sugar and beat well until combined for about 1 minute. Next add the cream and vanilla and beat until it's incorporated for another 1 to 2 minutes. Now start adding the eggs in one by one, mixing well in-between each addition, about 15 seconds each. Make sure you do not over mix it, or it will separate. Pour the batter into the cake pan and gently shake it to level it out. Place your cake pan into the larger baking dish. Pour hot water into the larger dish until it goes half-way up the side of the cake pan. (Make sure you don't splash water onto the cheesecake). Bake the cheesecake for 60 minutes or until the edges are slightly raised and the cake looks set. You can do a visual test to see if it's ready: Using oven mitts, jiggle the cake pan side to side. The center should still be a bit wobbly, but not liquid. If you have an oven thermometer, you can also test the doneness this way (the internal temperature should read 165°F [75°C]). Once the cheesecake is ready, take the cheesecake pan out of the baking dish. Turn the oven off and leave the cheesecake in the oven with the door open to prevent the cheesecake from cracking in the middle. Let it cool gradually for an hour. Then transfer the cheesecake to a wire rack. Run a knife all around the edges of the cheesecake to make sure it's not sticking. Wrap with plastic wrap and place in fridge for at least 5 to 6 hours. Once fully set, take out and remove the cheesecake from the tin.

(continued)

Kunafa Cheesecake (continued)

For the Kunafa Top Layer

3 oz (100 g) Kunafa dough (page 113)

¼ cup (50 g) butter, melted

For the Sugar Syrup

2 cups (400 g) granulated sugar

1 cup (240 ml) water

½ lemon, juiced

3 cardamom pods

For the Kunafa Bottom Layer

7 oz (250 g) Kunafa dough (page 113)

¼ cup (60 g) butter, melted

2 tbsp (30 g) granulated sugar

For Garnishing

Handful of crushed pistachios

1–2 tbsp (4–8 g) rose petals

For the kunafa top layer, break the kunafa dough by hand into small pieces. Place them in a pan over medium heat, then add the butter and cook until the shredded dough turns golden and crispy, about 12 to 15 minutes. Set it aside.

To make the sugar syrup, add the sugar, water, lemon juice and cardamom to a saucepan over medium heat and boil until it thickens for about 10 to 12 minutes. Set aside and let it cool completely.

When the cheesecake is done cooling, take it out of the oven and preheat the oven to 380°F (193°C). To prepare the kunafa bottom layer, mix the long stringy dough with butter and sugar. Coil the dough into a 10-inch (25-cm) cake pan like a snake until it covers the base completely. Then, using your fingers, press the dough down firmly so it holds. This serves as the sort of "crust" for the cheesecake. Place it in the oven and bake for 15 to 20 minutes, or until golden brown. While it's still hot, pour the sugar syrup on top.

To start layering, place the syrup-soaked bottom part of the kunafa on a large plate or cake stand as your base. Next, add the cheesecake and then the kunafa top layer. For the decoration, sprinkle the top with pistachios and rose petals. Serve with a cup of Qahwa (page 169).

Note: *Kuanafa cheesecake is best eaten the same day. Leftovers kept in air tight containers in the fridge can stay fresh for up to 4 to 5 days.*

Dates and Walnuts with Salted Caramel Cake

A lovely traditional Middle Eastern recipe that combines the sweetness of dates with the nuttiness of the walnuts and then topping it off with a silky, salty and buttery caramel that makes each bite simply divine.

Yield 8–10 Servings

For the Cake

6 oz (175 g) medjool dates, pitted

½ cup (100 g) granulated sugar

½ cup (115 g) unsalted butter, softened

1 egg

1¼ cups (300 ml) whole milk, lukewarm (110°F [43°C])

1¾ cups (240 g) flour, self-rising

1 tsp baking powder

½ tsp baking soda

½ tsp salt

¾ cup (60 g) cacao powder

½ tsp ground cinnamon

½ tsp ground cardamom

½ cup (60 g) walnuts, chopped

Melted butter for greasing

For the Salted Caramel

⅔ cup (140 g) brown sugar

½ cup (120 ml) whole milk

½ cup (120 ml) heavy cream

3-5 tbsp (45-75 g) unsalted butter

½ tsp vanilla extract

½ tsp salt

For Garnishing

½ cup (60 g) walnuts, chopped

To prepare the dates, soak the dates in boiling water for 5 minutes to soften them for the cake. Carefully remove the dates and squeeze all the water out. Then chop roughly and set aside.

To make the batter, first preheat the oven to 350°F (180°C). In a stand mixer bowl, beat the sugar and butter for 3 to 4 minutes on low speed using the wire whip attachment until fluffy and airy. Add the egg and milk, then whip for 1 to 2 minutes. In a large bowl, mix the flour, baking powder, baking soda, salt, cacao powder, cinnamon and cardamom. Add the dry mixture into the butter mixture and whisk for 2 minutes until well combined. Remove from the bowl from the stand mixer and add the walnuts and dates and mix gently using a spatula. Grease a 10-inch (25-cm) round pan with melted butter and add parchment paper to the bottom and the sides. Next, pour the mixture gently into the pan, tap it gently on the counter to remove any bubbles. Place it on the middle shelf of the oven and bake for 40 to 45 minutes or until golden. Take the cake out and place it on a rack and let it cool down completely (around 20 minutes) before flipping it over and removing the pan.

To make the caramel sauce, start by adding the sugar to a medium saucepan over medium heat and let it dissolve completely without ever moving it. Once all sugar has fully melted, slowly add the milk and whisk vigorously. Then add the cream, butter and vanilla and continue whisking until fully combined. Sprinkle the salt into the sauce, whisk slightly then set aside. Pour caramel on top of the cake, garnish with chopped walnuts and serve with ice cream if you like.

Note *Triple the amount of all ingredients if you plan on making it into a three-layered cake like the picture.*

Pistachio Cake

Pistachios have been growing in the Middle East for thousands of years. In this recipe I use them to make a lovely three-tier cake with a creamy frosting and a dash of ground pistachios all around. So, if you like pistachios as much as I do, then you need to give this recipe a try!

Yield 10–12 Servings

For the Cake

3⅔ cups (456 g) raw pistachios, divided

3½ cups (450g) all-purpose flour

1½ tbsp (21 g) baking powder

1½ tsp (7 g) baking soda

Pinch of salt

2¼ cups (450 g) granulated sugar

1½ cups (340 g) unsalted butter, softened

3 tsp (15 ml) vanilla extract

8 large eggs, room temperature

¾ cup (180 ml) Greek yogurt, room temperature

1½ cups (360 ml) whole milk, room temperature

For the Frosting

1½ cups (340 g) full fat cream cheese, softened

¾ cup (170 g) unsalted butter, softened

4 cups (500 g) powdered sugar

Pinch of salt

2 tsp (10 g) rose water (optional)

Note *You can opt for a two-layered cake instead of the three layers by reducing the quantity by one-third.*

Preheat oven to 350°F (180°C). Grease three 9-inch (22-cm) round cake pans with oil spray and a sprinkle of flour to coat. Then line the pans with parchment paper at the bottom and all around the edges and spray again with oil and set aside.

To make the cake, place the pistachios in a food processor and pulse until they are all ground and resemble breadcrumbs. Transfer 2½ cups (380 g) of the ground pistachios to a separate mixing bowl and reserve the remaining ½ cup (76 g) in a small cup for garnishing. Add flour, baking powder, baking soda and salt to the mixing bowl and set aside.

In a stand mixer bowl using the wire whip attachment, beat the sugar and butter until fluffy and creamy, around 3 to 4 minutes. Add the vanilla and the eggs, one at a time, and beat on high until fully combined, around 1 minute. Add the Greek yogurt and mix for another minute and while the mixer is on low speed, add the flour mixture alternating with the milk. Scrape down the sides of the bowl as needed. Pour the batter evenly into the cake pans and bake for around 21 to 24 minutes or until the cakes are baked all the way through. (You will know if they are fully baked by inserting a toothpick in the middle of the cake, if it turns out clean then the cake is ready). Take the cakes out and let them cool for at least 15 minutes before flipping them onto a wire rack, then let them cool completely before decorating with frosting.

To make the frosting, add the cream cheese and butter to a stand mixer bowl fitted with the wire whip attachment. Beat on high speed until smooth, creamy and there are no lumps, around 5 minutes. Add the powdered sugar and salt. If you are using rose water, you can add it now. Beat on low speed for 30 seconds, then switch to high speed and beat for 2 minutes.

To assemble the cake, place the first cake on a cake stand and add 4 to 5 tablespoons (60 to 75 g) of frosting on top. Then add the second cake and add another 4 to 5 tablespoons (60 to 75 g) of frosting. Lastly, add the third cake and spread the remaining two-thirds of the frosting, covering the cake completely using a straight spatula. Sprinkle the remaining pistachios all around the cake. Refrigerate for at least 30 to 45 minutes before slicing, then serve with Chai Bi Heil (page 166) or Karak Chai (page 168).

Almond Cake

This simple almond cake isn't super fancy or complex. It's rather a nostalgic kind of cake that my family liked to make. It's incredibly rich, moist and buttery, with an intense almond flavor. The caramel topping gives it a gooey finish and the flaked almonds give it a wonderful toasty crunch with every bite.

Yield 8–10 Servings

For the Topping

½ cup (75 g) almonds, blanched and halved

½ cup (114 g) butter

½ cup (100 g) granulated sugar

½ cup (113 ml) honey

For the Cake

⅔ cup (150 g) unsalted butter, softened and divided

2 cups (200 g) almond flour

1 cup (200 g) granulated sugar

1 tsp baking powder

1 tsp baking soda

Pinch of salt

4 eggs

1 tsp almond extract

1 tsp vanilla extract

½ cup (120 ml) full fat milk

Preheat your oven to 350°F (180°C).

To make the almond topping, scatter the almonds in a large skillet over low heat and toast until they turn a light golden color, around 4 to 6 minutes, tossing occasionally. Let them cool. Add the butter, sugar, honey and the toasted almonds to a medium-sized saucepan and cook for 5 or 6 minutes over medium heat or until the syrup slightly thickens and set aside.

To make the cake batter, grease a 9-inch (22-cm) cake pan with 1 tablespoon (15 g) of the softened butter, line with parchment paper rounds then grease the parchment paper and set aside. In a large bowl, add almond flour, sugar, baking powder, baking soda, salt and whisk well then set aside. In a stand mixer bowl, whisk the eggs, almond extract and the vanilla extract until fluffy. Gradually add the remainder of the butter and the milk and whisk for 2 minutes until fully combined. Slowly add in the almond flour mixture until it forms into a batter. Pour the batter into the cake pan and give it a light tap on the counter to release any air pockets.

Place it in the middle shelf of the oven and bake for 40 to 45 minutes. Take it out when a toothpick comes out clean when inserted into the cake. Let it cool on a wire rack for 15 minutes. Release it from the pan, top it with the almond caramel (you might need to slightly warm up the almond caramel if it's a bit thick), slice and serve with hot tea or Karak Chai (page 168).

Notes

- *You can store the cake for at least a week in the fridge. Just place it in an airtight container to maintain freshness.*
- *I prefer eating this cake warm. It tastes much better, especially with the almond nuts on top as it is nice and soft when warm. To serve warm, just place a slice in the microwave for 30 seconds before eating.*

Baghrir Cake with Rose Infused Frosting

Baghrir is known as the thousand-hole pancake, *due to the many air pockets that form on the face while cooking it in a pan. It is a Moroccan semolina pancake that is traditionally enjoyed with honey and butter syrup. They are delightfully sweet, spongy, light and fluffy. Since it is cooked on one side only, it can be eaten as a pancake soaked in a butter honey syrup or you can take it to the next level and make a cake with a smooth frosting all around.*

Yield 8–9 Pancakes

For the Frosting

¼ cup (50 g) cream cheese, softened

¼ cup (50 g) unsalted butter, softened

1⅔ cups (200 g) powdered sugar

1 tsp rose water

1 tbsp (15 g) rose petals, crushed

¼ cup (60 ml) heavy cream, chilled

For the Cake

1 tsp active dry yeast

1 tbsp (15 g) granulated sugar

2¼ cups (510 ml) water, lukewarm (110°F [43°C]), divided

1 cup (176 g) fine semolina

¼ cup (30 g) all-purpose flour

1 tsp baking powder

½ tsp salt

Rose petals, for garnish

To make the frosting, add the cream cheese and butter to a stand mixer bowl fitted with the wire whip attachment. Beat on high speed until smooth and creamy with no lumps, around 3 minutes. Add the powdered sugar and rose water and beat on low speed for 30 seconds. Switch to high speed and beat for another 2 minutes. Then add the rose petals, mix gently and set aside. In a separate bowl, whip the chilled heavy cream until it forms peaks. Fold it into the frosting and place in the fridge until it's ready to use.

To make the batter, in a small bowl, add the yeast, sugar and 4 table-spoons (60 ml) of lukewarm water. Whisk until it is fully dissolved. Let it proof for 10 minutes and set aside. In a blender, add the semolina flour, all-purpose flour, baking powder, salt, the yeast mixture and the remaining water. Blend for 1 to 2 minutes until homogenous. The result will be a thick and bubbly mixture. Transfer to a large bowl, cover with a kitchen towel and let it rest for 30 minutes.

Heat up a nonstick pan over medium to low heat. Ladle a scoop of batter into the pan. It will start to bubble instantly. Let the top cook completely and do NOT flip. Once they are cooked, place the baghrir on a kitchen towel side by side and do not stack them as they tend to stick together. Make sure to always keep them covered with a towel to prevent them from becoming dry.

To serve, place one baghrir on a large plate, then top it with 1 table-spoon (7 g) of frosting. Add the second baghrir and repeat the process until all baghrirs are stacked. Cover the last pancake with the remaining frosting and sprinkle with rose petals and place in the fridge. Serve with Chai Bi Ni'naa (page 167) or Qahwa (page 169).

Note *If no bubbles start popping when baking the pancakes, it is most likely that the batter is just too thick or that the batter has not had enough time to fully proof. Add 2 tablespoons (30 ml) of warm water to the batter and try again. Leave the batter to proof for an extra 15 minutes.*

Sponge Cake with Pomegranate Glaze

My mum was great at making cakes and even better at decorating them. Some days she would make an iced sugar cake and on other days, a simple yet delicious sponge cake. I remember helping my mum all the time when it came to cake—I would add the flour gradually and hope I didn't make a mess when pouring it into the mixer—and at the end of every cake, she would always leave me a bit of the batter in the mixing bowl. And now, after all these years, this recipe has become a staple in my family especially drizzled with a vibrant pomegranate glaze.

Yield 12 Servings

For the Cake

3¼ cups (400 g) all-purpose flour

1 tbsp (14 g) baking powder

Pinch of salt

1 cup (230 g) butter, softened

1½ cups (330 g) granulated sugar

5 medium eggs, room temperature

1 cup (240 ml) whole milk, room temperature

1 tsp vanilla extract

For the Pomegranate Glaze

2 cups (260 g) powdered sugar

5 tbsp (75 ml) pomegranate juice, freshly squeezed

Preheat oven to 350°F (180°C). Prepare a Bundt pan by spraying oil, covering it entirely, then sprinkling flour on top of the oil and then setting aside.

To prepare the batter, in a stand mixing bowl, sift the flour with the baking powder and salt and set aside.

In a separate stand mixing bowl, use the whisk attachment to whisk the butter and sugar together on medium speed, until creamy and fluffy, around 4 minutes. Add the eggs gradually one at a time until they are fully incorporated. Switch the speed to low speed and start adding about ¼ cup (30 g) of the flour mixture then ¼ cup (60 ml) of milk, alternating between them until all the flour and milk have been added. Lastly add the vanilla and whisk for 10 seconds more. Then pour the mixture into the Bundt pan and give it a light tap on the counter to release any air pockets. Bake in the oven for 48 to 55 minutes or until golden. To check if it's fully cooked, insert a toothpick inside the middle of the cake and if it comes out clean then your cake is ready. Take it out and let it cool for at least 30 minutes before flipping it on a wire rack. Let it cool completely before adding the icing.

To prepare the glaze, place the powdered sugar in a stand mixing bowl and using the whisk attachment on low speed, gradually add 1 tablespoon (15 ml) of the pomegranate juice at a time until the final texture is pourable and sticky. If it seems a bit runny, you can add more powdered sugar and if it's too thick add more pomegranate juice. Serve with Chai Bi Heil (page 166) or Karak Chai (page 168).

Qurs Akili Cake

Gers Ogel or Qors Oqaily is an exotic Arabian perfumed sponge cake from Kuwait infused with strong notes of saffron, cardamom and rose water. It is traditionally made from eggs, flour, sugar, cardamom and saffron with sesame seeds sprinkled on top and tahini paste on the bottom. It is traditionally served with sweetened milk tea or hot milk at breakfast. It is baked in the form of a disk hence the word gers *meaning disc. The word* ogaily *is derived from the traditional circular black rope-like shaped fabric or* ogal *that is worn on top of men heads in the Gulf region. It is extremely moist with a fluffy texture that will fill your home with a delicious aroma once baked.*

Yield 8 Servings

For the Cake

1 tsp saffron threads

1 cup (200 g) superfine granulated sugar, divided

¼ cup (60 ml) whole milk, warm

2 tbsp (30 ml) tahini (optional)

¼ cup (40 g) sesame seeds, slightly toasted, divided

3 cups (360 g) all-purpose flour

½ tbsp (3 g) ground cardamom

1 tsp baking powder

1 tsp salt

5 eggs, room temperature

1 tsp vanilla extract

½ cup (120 ml) vegetable oil

¾ cup (180 ml) whole milk, room temperature

1 tsp rose water (optional)

For Garnishing

¼ cup (30 g) powdered sugar (optional)

In a mortar, grind the saffron threads and 1 teaspoon of the sugar together. Then add the warm milk and set aside for 10 minutes. Prepare an 8-inch (20-cm) cake pan or a Bundt pan by greasing it with the tahini paste (if you are planning on using it) or just a spray of oil would suffice. Then sprinkle 2 tablespoons (20 g) of the toasted sesame seeds into the pan and set aside. We will be using the remaining 2 tablespoons (20 g) of sesame seeds at the end.

Preheat the oven to 350°F (180°C).

In a large bowl, sift the flour, cardamom, baking powder and salt and whisk until well combined. Set the dry mixture aside. In a stand mixing bowl, add the eggs, remaining sugar and vanilla and beat for 10 minutes until fluffy and foamy with a whisk. Then slowly add the vegetable oil while continuously whisking until it is combined. Then add the milk, saffron mixture and rose water (if you are using) and mix well. Then gently fold in the flour mixture using a spatula. Continue mixing until all ingredients are well combined. Pour it in the greased pan, sprinkle the remaining sesame seeds on top and bake it for 35 to 40 minutes or until the toothpick comes out clean when inserted into the cake. Place it on a wire rack and let it cool completely for at least 15 minutes. Then flip the cake onto a serving plate, sprinkle powdered sugar on top if desired. Slice and serve with Karak Chai (page 168) or hot milk.

Notes

- *Date molasses can be used as an alternative to sugar. Substitute with equal amounts.*
- *Qors Aqili can be served with whipped cream on top to give it a more layered flavor if desired.*

Khanfaroosh

Khanfaroush/Khanfaroosh is a Qatari mini, deep-fried, aromatic saffron and cardamom cake–also popular in the Emirates, Bahrain and Kuwait. It is made from a combination of rice flour and regular flour, infused with cardamom, saffron and rose water to give it a very unique flavor. Then it is deep-fried and dusted with powdered sugar or drizzled with honey. They are very soft and quite similar to donuts. Khanfaroush is typically paired with tea or Arabic coffee.

Yield 16–18 Pieces

For the Cake

½ tsp saffron threads

½ cup (100 g) superfine granulated sugar, divided

1 cup (160 g) rice flour

¾ cup (95 g) all-purpose flour

6 large eggs, beaten lightly

1 tsp ground cardamom

1 tsp baking powder

½ tsp salt

1 tsp rose water (optional)

For Frying

Vegetable oil

For Garnishing

¼ cup (30 g) powdered sugar

2 tbsp (14 g) ground pistachios (optional)

In a mortar, add the saffron threads and 1 teaspoon of the sugar and grind until it becomes a powder consistency and set aside. In a large bowl add in the remaining sugar, rice flour, all-purpose flour, eggs, cardamom, baking powder, salt and the ground saffron mixture. Add in the rose water if you choose to use it. Whisk well to form a smooth and thick batter then set aside for 30 minutes.

In a large deep-frying pan, add about a ¼ inch (5 mm) of oil. Place the pan over medium heat. Once it is hot, add ¼ cup (60 ml) of the batter into the oil. It will look like a pancake in shape but much smaller–only around 3 inches (8 cm). Let it fry for 1½ minutes or until golden. Then flip and cook on the other side too for another 1½ minutes. Take it out and place it on a plate lined with a paper towel to remove excessive oil. Once the oil has drained, transfer to a serving dish, dust with powdered sugar and sprinkle with ground pistachios (if using) and serve with Chai Aswad (page 165) or Qahwa (page 169).

Baklawa Cheesecake

If you love baklawa and you love cheesecake, then I'm sure you will love this. It combines the best of both worlds in one dessert—you get the crunchiness and the nuttiness from the baklawa, and you get the creaminess, smoothness and richness from the cheesecake. It might seem intimidating at first, but with my explicit instructions, it will be so easy to make and will be your new go-to dessert for family and friends' gatherings.

Yield 8 Servings

For the Honey Syrup

1 cup (200 g) granulated sugar

1½ cups (360 ml) water

1½ cups (340 ml) honey

For the Crust

⅓ cup (75 g) butter, melted, divided

15 phyllo dough sheets

½ cup (60 g) powdered sugar

3 cups (370 g) raw pistachios, toasted

Pinch of salt

For the Cheesecake

16 oz (500 g) cream cheese

1 cup (225 g) mascarpone cheese or Greek yogurt

¼ cup (60 ml) heavy cream

¼ cup (60 ml) honey

3 large eggs, room temperature

2 tsp (10 ml) vanilla extract

Pinch of salt

For Garnishing

⅔ cup (75 g) raw pistachios, ground

Handful of rose petals

To prepare the honey syrup, add the sugar and water to a medium-sized pot and let it boil for 15 minutes. Once it has thickened slightly, add the honey, mix to combine and set aside.

Preheat the oven to 350°F (180°C).

Prepare an 8-inch (20-cm) cheesecake pan by brushing the inside with melted butter. Place two phyllo dough sheets into the bottom of the pan, so that both edges of the sheet are slightly hanging off the edge of the pan. Next, brush the sheets with melted butter. Add two more sheets on the opposite side while both edges are also dangling on the side of the pan. Repeat this process, layering the sheets one on top of the other, until ten sheets have been added.

In a bowl, mix three-quarters of the remaining butter with the powdered sugar, pistachios and salt, then spread evenly on top of the layered phyllo sheets. Using your fingers, press down gently but firmly. Add five more phyllo sheets while brushing them with the remaining butter in between and then set aside.

To make the cheesecake filling, in a stand mixer bowl add the cream cheese and mascarpone (or Greek yogurt if you are choosing to use it). Using the whisk attachment, whisk the cheese until creamy. Next, add the heavy cream and whisk for another 2 to 3 minutes. Then add the honey and whisk for an additional 2 minutes. Lastly add the eggs, vanilla and salt and whisk until fully combined. Pour the cheesecake batter on top of the nut mixture and bake for 1 hour to 1 hour and 10 minutes or until the cheesecake is fully cooked. The center should still be a bit wobbly but not liquid. The internal temperature should be 165°F (75°C). Let it cool completely in the oven after turning the oven off and opening the oven door. Let it gradually cool down so the cheesecake doesn't crack in the middle then place it in the fridge for at least 2 hours to chill. Take the cheesecake out just before serving and garnish with pistachios and rose petals. Slice and enjoy with Chai Bi Heil (page 166).

Note *You can use ½ cup (100 g) granulated sugar or powdered sugar instead of honey in the cheesecake recipe.*

Fig Jam Cold Cheesecake

One of our neighbors back home in Baghdad had a huge fig tree that had large branches hanging all over our side of the wall. I would go upstairs to the second floor and jump out onto the balcony just so I could pick a few. I would sit there eating them while enjoying the view from that height. I remember them to be extremely sweet with a soft, furry type of skin. My mom would also occasionally ask me to go pick some whenever she needed them in her dishes. So, this recipe was made in memory of that time and those moments I would daydream, sitting on the edge of that balcony.

Yield 8 Servings

For the Base Layer

30 full sheets (500 g) graham crackers

1 cup (227 g) butter, softened

For the Cheesecake

1¼ cups (300 ml) heavy cream

2½ cups (600 g) cream cheese

1 cup (120 g) powdered sugar

1 tsp vanilla extract

For Garnishing

10-15 figs, diced

1 cup (120 g) powdered sugar

1½ cups (250 g) fresh figs, quartered

Rosemary sprigs

¼ cup (30 g) pistachios, whole

To make the base layer, add the graham crackers to a food processor and process until they are fine. Then add the butter and process until the texture resembles breadcrumbs. Add the cracker mixture to a 9-inch (22-cm) cheesecake pan and press gently but firmly to create a base for the cheesecake. Place the pan in the freezer for at least 1 hour.

To make the cheesecake, add the heavy cream into a stand mixer bowl and whisk until peaks start to form. Then add the cream cheese and whisk again until fully combined and thick. Lastly add the powdered sugar and vanilla and whisk for another 2 to 4 minutes. Set aside.

Take the pan out of the freezer and add the cream cheese mixture and spread evenly using a spatula. Cover with a plate or loose plastic wrap (making sure it doesn't touch the cheesecake). Place in the freezer overnight to set.

The next day, once the cheesecake is set, it's time to prepare the fig jam. First add the figs with the powdered sugar to a saucepan and let it boil over medium heat while stirring occasionally. Let it cook gently for 15 to 20 minutes or until the quantity has been reduced to two-thirds and the consistency is thick like a jam. Remove from heat and let it cool completely. Take out the cheesecake from the freezer, add the jam on top and let it thaw for 30 minutes before garnishing. To garnish, add sliced figs, rosemary sprigs and sprinkle pistachios on top. Slice and serve while cold.

Note *Cold cheesecake needs to stay in the fridge or even better in the freezer. If you choose to freeze it, it will require around 30 minutes to thaw before serving.*

Lazy Cake

Chocolatey, crunchy and buttery lazy cake is one of my favorite go-to cakes that I like to make for my family when I don't have much time to dedicate to making a cake. It is called "lazy" because it's no-bake, takes less than 15 minutes to make and only requires 5 ingredients! It is sometimes referred to as a biscuit cake or chocolate biscuit cake and tends to only use tea biscuits—a favorite for grownups and kids alike. It is even better the next day, as the biscuit starts to soften and fully absorb the rest of the ingredients.

Yield 8–10 Servings

For the Cake

6 cups (500 g) tea biscuits

1½ cups (230 g) 70% cacao dark chocolate, melted

2 cups (200 g) cocoa powder

2¾ cups (790 g) sweetened condensed milk

1 cup (227g) unsalted butter, melted

For Garnishing

2 cups (475 g) 70% dark chocolate, melted

Using your hands, break the tea biscuits into medium-sized pieces and place into a large bowl. (The pieces don't have to be uniform in size).

In a separate bowl, add the melted dark chocolate, cocoa powder, sweetened condensed milk and melted butter. Whisk everything together until it's fully combined.

Pour the chocolate mixture over the crushed biscuits and combine using a spatula until all the biscuits are covered in chocolate.

Line a 12-inch (30-cm) cheesecake pan with parchment paper. Then add the chocolate biscuit mixture. Press and pack it firmly into the pan. (Do not worry if the biscuits break). To garnish, add the melted chocolate on top. Then, cover it with plastic wrap, making sure it doesn't touch the chocolate surface. Place the pan in the freezer and freeze for 2 to 3 hours or until set. To serve, cut slices of lazy cake using a bread knife for a neat slice and serve with Chai Aswad (page 165).

Notes

- *You can use whatever chocolate you prefer. It can be semi-dark or even milk chocolate.*
- *The cake can be kept at room temperature for 3 to 5 days.*

Biscuits, Cookies and Bites

Small treats are the favorite kind of sweets in Middle Eastern and North African cuisine, as they can easily accompany a cup of tea or coffee. Creating some of these cookies and biscuits holds very fond memories of making them with my mom and sister in the kitchen—at the kitchen table amongst family members. Large batches are usually made so they can be shared with other family members and neighbors. You would frequently see full plates of *Kleicha* (page 67) or *Ghuraibah* (page 78) going out to the neighbor and a full plate of a different kind of cookie coming back. Generosity goes both ways, and everyone wants to share their homemade cookies and biscuits—especially during festive periods. In this chapter, I'm sharing some of those recipes (and more) that can be enjoyed with a warm cup of tea.

Kleicha

Kleicha is a very traditional Iraqi sweet that is usually prepared on Eid celebrations, and it is in fact its national cookie. It is a soft buttery dough that comes in several shapes and fillings. While date filling is more popular, other fillings can be made from crushed sugared walnuts, shredded coconut and more. This recipe explores the date stuffed one. I remember my mom making these all the time growing up. The aroma of fresh baked dough with an infused smell of butter and a hint of cardamom was pure heaven. That divine smell would fill the house for hours after and now that I have kids of my own, I am carrying on with that tradition. Seeing my kids experience the exact same thing I did at their age truly fills my heart with joy.

Yield 10–12 Servings

For the Dough

2 tsp (7 g) active dry yeast

2 tsp (8 g) granulated sugar

¼ cup (60 ml) water, lukewarm (110°F [43°C])

5¼ cups (690 g) all-purpose flour

1 tsp salt

1 cup (227 g) unsalted butter, softened

1 cup (240 ml) whole milk, lukewarm (110°F [43°C])

For the Date Filling

3 tbsp (45 g) butter

2 cups (350 g) medjool dates, pitted

2 tsp (3 g) ground cardamom

For Glaze

1 egg

Note *You can make the kleicha smaller or bigger depending on the thickness you will be slicing them. I like them on the smaller side, but feel free to explore to your liking.*

Preheat oven to 380°F (195°C)

To prepare the dough start by adding yeast, sugar and warm water into a bowl. Set aside to rise for up to 10 minutes. In a stand mixer bowl, add the flour, salt and yeast mixture and mix for 30 seconds. Then add the butter and mix again on medium speed for 2 minutes or until the mixture forms into a breadcrumb like texture. Gradually add the milk until it starts to form a dough, around 2 to 3 minutes. Cover the bowl with plastic wrap and cover it with a warm towel. Leave it aside for a couple of hours.

To prepare the dates, place a saucepan on the stove over medium heat. Add the butter and once it has melted, add the dates and cardamom. Start squashing them with a spatula until they form into a dough, around 10 minutes. Remove from the heat and let it cool down for 10 minutes.

To start assembling the kleicha, take the rested dough out of the bowl and cut it in half. Place one of the halves on an oiled surface and start spreading it using a rolling pin into a rectangular shape until it becomes thin (less than ¼ inch [5 mm] thickness). Cut the rectangular dough into three even pieces. Spread the date mixture gently using your fingers to spread evenly over all 3 pieces, forming a thin layer, leaving only a ½ inch (10 mm) space on one end of the dough. Then begin to roll all 3, one by one, like a Swiss roll starting from the opposite side to the edge with the ½-inch (10-mm) space. Once fully rolled, use a knife to cut 1- to 1½-inch (2.5- to 4-cm) slices and place them on a greased baking tray. Repeat the process for the other half of the dough.

In a small bowl, whisk the egg and then brush each slice evenly with the egg wash. Place the tray in the middle of the oven for 20 to 22 minutes or until golden. Enjoy it warm with Chai Aswad (page 165) or Chai Bi Heil (page 166).

Maamoul

These buttery, flaky stuffed cookies are very popular in many Middle Eastern countries like Syria, Palestine, Lebanon and many more. They literally melt in your mouth. The actual cookie is mild in sweetness; it relies only on its stuffing component for its sweetness. They are considered the sister cookie of Kleicha (page 67) but kleicha is more doughy, less flaky and made only with flour. Maamoul can also be stuffed with a variety of other fillings like dates, pistachios or walnuts.

Yield 14-16 Cookies

For the Dough

1¼ cups (155g) fine semolina

1½ cups (180 g) all-purpose flour

1 tsp mahlab

1 tsp ground anise

1 tsp fennel

½ cup (90 g) ghee, melted and warm

¼ cup (60 g) unsalted butter, melted and warm

1 tsp salt

2 tsp (30 g) granulated sugar

3 tbsp (50 ml) full fat milk, warmed

1 tsp orange blossom or rose water (optional)

For the Date Stuffing

1⅓-1½ cups (350 g–450 g) Mejdool dates, pitted

2 tbsp (30 g) butter

1 tsp ground cardamom

Powdered sugar, for garnish

To prepare the dough, in a large bowl, add the semolina, flour, mahlab, anise and fennel and give it a gentle mix. Then pour in the melted ghee, butter, salt and sugar and mix well for up to 5 minutes. Add the milk and orange blossom or rose water (if using). Mix one more time, then cover with plastic wrap and let it rest for 1 hour at room temperature.

Start preparing the date stuffing by placing the dates, butter and cardamom in a pan over medium heat. Mix well using a spatula until it forms into a thick paste, which takes around 10 minutes. Set it aside to cool down completely.

Preheat the oven to 350F (180C).

To assemble the cookies, take your rested dough and divide it into 35 to 40 gram balls (around 14 to 16 balls). Place the dough balls on a baking sheet. Prepare a second sheet and repeat the process using the date paste but only using 20 to 25 grams of the paste to form the balls. Using you palms, squash each dough ball to flatten it out as much as you can. Add the date ball in the middle and wrap the dough around, making sure the date paste is fully covered. Position the ball in a floured maamoul mold. Press firmly but gently, until it makes a clean impression. Remove from the mold by smacking it gently on the palm of your hand, then place on an oiled baking sheet. Repeat with the rest of the dough balls, making sure you flour the mold before every use.

Bake in the middle of the oven for 10 to 14 minutes, then broil on low for 2 minutes to give it a golden color. Transfer the cookies to a wire rack and let them cool completely. Dust them with powdered sugar and serve with Qahwa (page 169) or Chai Aswad (page 165).

Note *Although molds are preferred, you can still shape it using a fork. As soon as the date balls are fully covered with the dough, move it between your palms to form a ball, place it on the baking dish and press gently to flatten it out. Use the tip of the fork to make dents in it before placing it in the oven to bake.*

Barazek

Barazek are delicious Syrian cookies that are made primarily from flour and ghee. Instead of using a rolling pin to spread the dough, fingers are used to press the balls gently into toasted sesame seeds on one side, and finely crushed pistachios on the other side. This makes them light and crispy with a nutty flavor to them. They can also be a bit chewy, which is achieved by not flattening out the dough too much. Barazek are considered one of the most famous Syrian desserts and they do have a lot of variants—like adding eggs to the mixture, yeast or butter instead of ghee, honey or date paste is also used instead of regular sugar syrup. And although these cookies originated from Syria, they can also be found throughout the Levant region (Lebanon, Jordan and Palestine) with a similar recipe.

Yield 35 Cookies

½ cup (72 g) sesame seeds

2½ cups (310 g) all-purpose flour

1 tsp mahlab (optional)

Pinch of salt

½ cup (125 g) ghee, cold

⅓ cup (80 ml) water

⅓ cup (75 g) granulated sugar

2 tsp (9 g) baking powder

In a large pan over medium to low heat, add the sesame seeds and toast. This process will take around 12 to 15 minutes while constantly moving the sesame seeds around to prevent toasting them too much. As soon as you notice a light golden color, remove them immediately and place in a bowl, then set aside.

To make the dough, in a stand mixer bowl and using the whisk attachment, add the flour, mahlab (if using), salt and cold ghee. Mix on low to medium speed until well combined, around 3 minutes. Then let it rest for 5 to 10 minutes

In a separate bowl, add the water, sugar, baking powder and whisk until the sugar has been completely dissolved. Then pour it on top of the flour mixture and using the dough hook attachment, mix gently on low until the dough has absorbed all the sugar mixture (around 2 minutes). As soon as you notice the sugar is well combined, turn the mixer off as we do not want it to over mix (to not activate the gluten). It should look like whipped cream. Next, using your hand (preferably wearing a glove), bring the dough together until it forms into a super soft dough. Transfer it to a bowl and place, uncovered, in the fridge for 2 to 3 hours (you can place it in the freezer for 30 minutes instead if you are in a hurry).

(continued)

Notes

- *The sesame seeds should only be toasted lightly in the pan and with a very light golden color. If they are toasted more than that, they will burn when baking the cookies and as a result, the taste will become bitter.*

- *The thinner you make the cookies, the crunchier they are. But keep in mind that they will bake faster, so reduce baking time. However, if you like them to be chewier then don't press it too much before baking.*

Barazek (continued)

For the Topping

1 tbsp (15 ml) sugar syrup

1 tbsp (15 g) granulated sugar

⅔ cup (75 g) raw pistachios, finely crushed

Just before taking the dough out, place the toasted sesame seeds in a deep baking tray. Make sure it is still warm before adding the sugar syrup and sugar (as the sugar might become hard) and using your hands (preferably wearing disposable gloves as they will start to stick to your hand), rub the sugar in the sesame seeds until it has been fully absorbed. To make sure that the texture is correct, press your hand in the sesame seed mixture and if the sesame seeds stick to your hand, then you are good to go. If it doesn't stick, then just add 1 tablespoon (15 ml) more of sugar syrup and mix. Now, take the dough out of the fridge. It will be slightly rough but easy to shape. The colder the dough is the more it will hold its shape, especially when flattening them out. Place the pistachios on a separate baking sheet.

Before you begin shaping your cookies, preheat the oven to 350°F (180°C).

Start shaping the dough into small balls about 2 inches (5 cm) big and ⅓ to ½ oz (10 to 15 g) in weight. They are relatively small, but you can increase the size if you want to 3 inches (8 cm). Take one ball and press down gently into the sesame seed mixture. Then flip it on the other side and press down with your fingers into the pistachio mixture. This is the step where you will flatten it out to the desired 2-inch (5-cm) size disc. Make sure not to press too much as the pistachios might pierce right through the dough. Once both sides are coated, take it out and place it on a baking sheet lined with parchment paper. Repeat the process for all the balls, making sure there is at least a 1 inch (2.5 cm) space in between. Place the cookies in the middle rack in the oven and bake for 8 minutes or until golden. Broil it for another 2 minutes if you like the sesame seeds to be more toasted and for the cookies to have a more golden appearance. Once they are ready, take them out and place on a cooling rack. Serve with Chai Bi Ni'naa (page 167) or Qahwa (page 169).

Notes

- *If you increase the size of the cookie to 3 inches (8 cm) and around ¾ ounce (25 g) in weight, then you will need an extra 3 to 6 minutes in the oven. The total quantity of the biscuits in this size is 18 pieces.*

- *Barazek can be stored in an airtight container in the fridge or even on the counter for 3 to 5 days.*

- *If the sesame mixture becomes hard, preheat in the oven for 3 to 5 minutes.*

Kaak Al Asawir

Kaak al asawar means bracelet cookies and is also known as kaak bi ajwa *or cookies with dates. It is a Palestinian cookie stuffed with date paste. It is made in the shape of bracelet and baked especially during Ramadan. It is delightfully soft from the inside but crunchy from the outside. What makes Kaak al asawir unique is the spices that are added to its dough which is a mixture of ground anise and ground fennel. This addition of spices will smell like licorice and your entire house will smell amazing for hours after baking these delectable bracelets.*

Yield 10–12 Bracelets

For the Filling

3 cups (550 g) medjool dates, pitted

5 tbsp (35 g) butter or ghee, melted

1 tsp ground cardamom

For the Dough

2 tbsp (12 g) anise seeds

2 tbsp (12 g) fennel seeds

1 tsp active dry yeast

2 tsp (8 g) granulated sugar

1½ cups (360 ml) water, lukewarm (110°F [43°C]), divided

3 cups (360 g) all-purpose flour

1 cup (175 g) fine semolina

1 tsp baking powder

1 tsp baking soda

½ cup (60 g) milk powder

½ cup (60 g) powdered sugar

3 tbsp (30 g) sesame seeds, preferably toasted

3 tbsp (10 g) black seeds or Nigella seeds

½ cup + 2 tbsp (150 ml) vegetable oil

½ cup (115 g) ghee, melted

To prepare the filling, add the dates to a large pan with the butter and cardamom over low to medium heat. Mix and combine gently until it becomes a soft mixture and a shiny dough, around 10 to 15 minutes. Take 1½ tablespoons (10 to 15 g) of the date mixture and form small balls. Repeat the process for all the remaining paste then set it aside. Make sure the paste remains warm so you can easily spread it.

To prepare the dough, start by grinding both the anise and fennel in a clean coffee grinder (or mortar and pestle), then set aside. Add the yeast, sugar and ¼ cup (60 ml) of the warm water to a small bowl and let it proof for 10 minutes. In a large mixing bowl, add flour, semolina, ground fennel and anise along with baking powder, baking soda and the yeast mixture. Mix well with a spatula until everything is well combined. Next add the milk powder, powdered sugar, sesame seeds, black seeds, vegetable oil and ghee. Mix well until it starts looking like wet breadcrumbs. Then add the remaining water gradually while mixing and knead gently for 2 to 3 minutes, until it forms into a dough. Do not over work the dough as we do not want the gluten to develop. Let it rest for 10 minutes.

Preheat your oven to 350°F (180°C).

After the dough has rested, start shaping the dough by taking 2 tablespoons (30 to 35 g) of the dough and form into balls. Repeat the process with the remaining dough.

(continued)

Kaak Al Asawir (continued)

Oil your hands and take one dough ball and shape it into a 1 x 8-inch (2.5 x 20-cm) log by rolling it across your work surface. Flatten it with your palms into a rectangular shape. Take one of the date balls and form into a log shape that is 1 inch (2.5 cm) shorter than the dough. Place it in the center of the dough. Then wrap the dough around it by pinching both longer sides then sealing the other until you have a cylinder shape. Roll it gently to ensure it is fully sealed, then take both ends and seal them together by placing one on top of the other and pressing. (It will look dented but that is what it should look like). Your cookies should now have the appearance of a bracelet. Place them on a baking sheet with parchment paper then bake in the oven for 12 to 14 minutes or until golden. You can broil it for 3 to 4 minutes if you want that extra golden color. Take them out and place them on a cooling rack. Serve with Qahwa (page 169) for the authentic experience.

Notes

- *You can use readymade store-bought date paste. Just warm 1¼ pounds (500 g) of it in the microwave. Add it to a bowl then add 2 tablespoons (30 g) of butter and 1 teaspoon of cardamom. Mix well until fully combined, soft and shiny.*

- *You can use warm milk instead of warm water if you like it to be doughier and softer.*

- *To prevent the biscuits from browning at the bottom, add another baking sheet underneath the one holding the biscuits.*

Coconut Cookies

This was the very first recipe that I learned about shaved coconut and how good it is. This recipe is relatively easy to make with minimal ingredients to highlight the taste of the coconut. It's like a Raffaello minus the white chocolate. I sometimes like dipping them in melted chocolate at the end but that's just me!

Yield 18–22 Balls

3 egg whites

½ cup (100 g) granulated sugar

2 cups (200 g) sweetened shredded coconut

2½ cups (250 g) unsweetened shredded coconut

1 tsp baking powder

1 tsp vanilla extract

¾ cup (90 g) powdered milk

Preheat oven to 370°F (190°C).

In a large bowl, add the egg whites and with a hand mixer, beat the eggs until stiff peaks are formed, around 10 minutes. To the whipped egg, add the sugar, both shredded coconuts, baking powder, vanilla extract and milk powder. Mix with a spatula until well combined. Set it aside for 10 minutes.

Prepare a baking sheet by lining it with parchment paper. Take the coconut mixture and start forming small balls around 1 to 1½ ounces (30 to 40 g). Place the balls on the baking sheet and place in the fridge for 20 minutes. Once firm, place them in the oven for 14 to 18 minutes or until golden. Take the cookies out and let them cool completely before removing them from the oven sheet. Serve with Karak Chai (page 168) or Chai Bi Heil (page 166).

Note *Coconut balls need to be kept in air tight containers as exposure to air will make them sticky.*

Ghuraibah

This is a very traditional dessert that you can find in most Middle Eastern households, especially Iraq, Palestine, Lebanon and the Levant area. It is made from flour, melted ghee and powdered sugar. It has a very flaky texture that literally melts in your mouth. It was first made from almond flour but now it's more popular to use regular wheat flour instead. My mom was always making them in huge batches, filling the house with the sweet cardamom aroma and then putting them in large ziplock bags and stacking them into the freezer for later use. They didn't last long either! She would always take a few out to warm them up and serve it with black tea. I may or may not have sneaked some out of the freezer without her knowing. In my defense—they were just too tempting and hard to resist!

Yield 35–40 Cookies

4 cups (500 g) all-purpose flour

1⅓ cups (160 g) powdered sugar

1 tsp ground cardamom

Pinch of salt

1¼ cups (280 g) ghee or clarified butter, softened

For Garnishing

⅔ cup (75 g) pistachios

In a stand mixer bowl, sift the flour and powdered sugar into the bowl. Add the cardamom, salt and the ghee and using the paddle attachment, mix on low to medium speed for 10 minutes. It will start out very crumbly but will gradually transform to a thick icing cream-like texture. Continue mixing for another 5 minutes to ensure there are no lumps and the mixture becomes very smooth and silky. It should be like a thick batter and not like dough so do not be tempted to add any extra flour.

Add parchment paper to two large baking sheets. Prepare a piping bag with a large round tip. I used an Ateco 809 plain tip which creates a smooth, wide dollop. Add the mixture to the piping bag, twist the end and start piping onto one of the baking sheets. This might require a bit of practice to get them to look similar but once you get the hang of it, it will be relatively easy. Make sure when you are piping that there is at least 1½ inch (4 cm) space in between.

To flatten the cookies, dip a finger in flour then gently tap on the peak to flatten it and create a slight dent then add a pistachio in it. Repeat the process until you run out. Place the baking sheets in the fridge so the biscuits become firmer and less sticky, around 30 minutes.

Take the baking sheets out and preheat the oven to 250°F (120°C). Bake for 16 to 18 minutes. The biscuits should maintain their white color with no browning on the bottom. Once they are ready, take them out. They will leave a residue on your finger if you touch them but don't worry, they are fully cooked. The cookies need to cool for at least 2 hours to overnight before placing them in an airtight container.

Simsimiya

Simsimiya takes me back to my childhood. As I remember my mum making them as kids, I would get excited seeing them on the kitchen table and would have to help myself to a few pieces. I've come to learn later on that there are so many varieties of them throughout Middle East and North African countries. But they all are made with 5 ingredients or less to create that perfectly sweet, nutty and crunchy dessert and that makes it a winner in my book.

Yield 15–20 Pieces

1½ cups (215 g) white sesame seeds

1 cup (260 g) granulated sugar

4 tbsp (60 ml) honey

1 tsp vanilla extract

Toast the sesame seeds in a pan over low heat for 6 to 8 minutes stirring frequently until golden. Transfer seeds to a bowl and let them cool down completely. Place the sugar in a big saucepan over medium-low heat without stirring until completely melted. Now you can add the honey and once the mixture has reached an amber color, remove completely from the heat. Add the sesame seeds and vanilla and mix well.

Grease a 9 x 12-inch (22 x 30-cm) pan and line with parchment paper. Next, pour in the mixture and let it cool down for a couple of minutes. Once it has cooled, oil your hands (with a neutral oil like canola) and gently but firmly press on the sesame dough to spread it evenly into the pan. You can use a spatula, but I find that hands do a better job. While still warm, cut into 1-inch (2.5-cm) pieces or bigger if you like. To keep the candies from sticking together, place them in the freezer and leave them there for 20 minutes. Take them out and place on a serving tray with Chai Bi Heil (page 166) or Qahwa (page 169).

Notes

- *You can use parchment paper instead of your hands. Simply place it on top of the sesame mixture and using a rolling pin, spread evenly.*

- *Simsimiya with honey is best kept in the fridge as it tends to stick together if left outside. You can omit the honey for a harder, less sticky result and increasing the sugar by 2 tablespoons (30 g).*

- *If you like Simsimiya to be on the chewier side, increase the quantity of the honey by 3 tablespoons (50 ml) and reduce the sugar by ¼ cup (50 g).*

Date Balls

This is one of my favorite desserts that has only two main ingredients with your choice of garnish. You can roll the balls in crushed nuts, melted chocolate, toasted sesame seeds or sweet shaved coconut. My mum would always make these whenever she had leftover filling from making a huge batch of Kleicha (page 67). It is easy, fast and extremely satisfying, especially with a cup of warm cardamom black tea.

Yield 20–25 Balls

For the Date Balls

3 cups (540 g) medjool dates, pitted

⅓ cup (75 g) butter

For Garnishing

⅔ cup (75 g) crushed pistachios or crushed cashews (90 g)

¼ cup (40 g) toasted sesame seeds

½ cup (48 g) sweetened shredded coconut

½ cup (70 g) pine nuts, toasted

½ cup (50 g) unsweetened cocoa powder

Remove the pits from all dates and place all the dates in a large pan over medium heat. Add the butter and with a spatula, start squashing the dates with the butter until it starts to form into a paste, around 10 to 12 minutes. Once fully combined and the dough looks very shiny, remove from heat and place in a large bowl and let it cool completely.

Line a baking sheet with parchment paper. Place pistachios (or cashews), sesame seeds, coconut, pine nuts and cocoa powder in separate bowls. Once the date paste has cooled down, take about 1 tablespoon (15 g) of the mixture and form it into a ball. Place it on parchment paper and repeat the process for all the remaining paste. Roll balls in your chosen garnish or leave them plain! Serve with a side of tahini paste for dipping.

Note *Size of balls is based on your preference. You can go with a slightly larger 2 tablespoons (30 g) in size.*

Baid Al Qata

Baid al qata or salouq *is a very traditional Kuwaiti dessert that goes back hundreds of years. The name translates to "eggs of Qata" which is a rare bird called* sangrouse *that is very popular in the Gulf region. They are small, delicious bites stuffed with a nut mixture then deep-fried and covered with powdered sugar to give it that extra deliciousness. They definitely remind me of donuts minus the filling.*

Yield 11-13 Pieces

For the Dough

2 cups (260 g) all-purpose flour

1 tsp ground cardamom

1 tsp baking powder

1 tsp baking soda

1 tsp salt

¼ cup (50 g) butter, melted

¼ cup (50 g) ghee, melted

1 tsp saffron soaked in 1 tbsp (15 ml) rose water

½ cup (120 ml) whole milk, lukewarm (110°F [43°C])

For the Filling

2 cups (240 g) walnuts, crushed

2 tbsp (30 g) granulated sugar

1 tsp ground cardamom

1 tsp ground cinnamon

For Frying

1 quart (960 ml) vegetable oil

For Garnishing

3¼ cups (400 g) powdered sugar

For the dough, sift the flour into a stand mixing bowl. Then add cardamom, baking powder, baking soda, salt and mix. Next add the butter and ghee. Using the dough hook, mix for 1 minute until well combined. Add the saffron water and gradually add the milk while mixing until the dough starts to take shape. You might not need all the milk so as soon as it comes together and is not sticky, stop pouring the milk. Set it aside and let it rest for 1 hour.

In a separate bowl, mix the walnuts, sugar, cardamom and cinnamon and blend well. Set this mixture aside. Start shaping the balls by taking 2 to 3 tablespoons (35 to 40 g) of the dough and using your palms to roll it into balls. Repeat until you have 11 to 13 balls. Take a ball and use your palms to flatten it out. Take approximately 1 tablespoon (15 to 20 g) of the walnut mixture and place it in the center. While holding on to the edges, seal the edges by folding them one on top of the other. Shape the ball with both your hands into an egg-like shape. Place them on a baking sheet lined with parchment paper and place in the fridge for at least 30 minutes.

Place a deep pot over medium-high heat and add the oil. Once it reaches 365°F (185°C), add the balls gradually, making sure you do not add more than 4 to 5 at the same time (depending on the size of the pot). Let them cook for 1 minute on each side until they are golden brown. Then flip them over and cook for another minute. Reduce the heat slightly and continue deep frying all the balls. Place them on a wire rack to remove excess oil. While they are still hot, toss them in a bowl with the powdered sugar and let it soak in there for a minute. Once they are coated, take them out and place them in a serving dish. Serve with Qahwa (page 169).

Note *Baid al qata can be baked in an oven or in an air fryer. They will tend to be a bit harder than the soft ones that are deep-fried in oil, but they will cut down on the calories from the oil. Bake or air fry them at 350°F (180°C) for 10 minutes or until golden.*

Phyllo My Heart

My first time using this paper-thin pastry dough to make baklawa was quite disastrous. I had no clue what I was doing or how to properly use it. I couldn't recall seeing my mum using it when making her famous baklawa and only remember seeing her holding the pan after it being baked. So instead of just calling her like an adult to learn how to properly use it, I thought I could easily handle it myself. Little did I know that it wasn't that easy without some guidance. The dough was extremely delicate and instead of folding the dough to fit the pan I was using, I would cut the extra dough and throw the remainder away. That really was an unforgivable rookie mistake, but I've come to learn how to accurately use it now. I've really come a long way from those early days and now I can say proudly that I've mastered the way of handling and using phyllo in any recipe I want. Using phyllo can help you create the most delicious desserts you could ever taste. It's like puff pastry but not exactly. It has the flakiness of it, the butter in between and the multiple layers too but the results here are much lighter, airier and extremely crunchy—even after being soaked with sugar syrup like My Mum's Baklawa (page 89) or the Asawir Il Sit (page 96) that are so decadent and addictive. I can confidently say that you will be back for seconds.

My Mum's Baklawa

Growing up in the U.K., I remember my mum always making baklawa when we had people over. She would use a large round pan, add the soft layers of phyllo pastry and a thick layer of crushed walnuts in between. She would drizzle warm butter then bake it until it was crisp and flaky. She would then drizzle the cardamom-infused simple sugar syrup on top as soon as it was out of the oven—what a sensational sizzling sound that would make! Our guests would wait anxiously for it and every time my mum would bring that large pan out, it would receive a huge standing ovation. At that young age of six, I never quite understood the commotion surrounding it. But now that I'm older (and hopefully wiser), I understand why this simple but yet elegant dessert deserved all that and much more. It truly is a masterpiece of design and flavor!

Yield 10 Servings

3¼ cups (380 g) crushed walnuts

1 cup (200 g) granulated sugar

Avocado oil spray

1 (16-oz [454-g]) package phyllo dough, thawed

1 cup (230g) unsalted butter, melted

Preheat the oven to 300°F (160C).

In a large bowl, mix the crushed walnuts with the granulated sugar until well combined. Set this aside. Spray the avocado oil into a 12-inch (30-cm) round pan. Place two sheets of the dough into the pan, folding any extra dough inwards. Then spray the top completely with the avocado oil. Place another two pieces of the dough and repeat the process until you have ten phyllo sheets in total. Spread half of the nut mixture evenly over the base layer of phyllo dough. Add another eight layers of the dough, spraying every two layers with the avocado oil. Add the remaining half of the nut mixture. Then top it off with twelve more layers of phyllo dough, spraying avocado oil every two layers. Lastly, spray the top of the baklawa with oil, just before cutting to prevent the top layer from moving. With a sharp knife, cut straight and diagonal slices, all the way through creating diamond shaped pieces. You can also adopt the cutting in the photos below, if you want to be adventurous. Drizzle the melted butter on top evenly and though all the cuts. Bake for 1 hour and 15 minutes or until the top is golden.

(continued)

My Mums baklawa (continued)

For the Simple Syrup

2 cups (400 g) granulated sugar

1 cup (240 ml) water

3–4 cardamom pods

1 tsp fresh lemon juice

For Garnishing

Ground walnuts or pistachios

Dried rose petals (optional)

While the baklawa is baking, we are going to prepare the sugar syrup. Add the sugar and water to a medium sized saucepan over medium heat. Let it boil until all the sugar has been fully dissolved, around 7 to 10 minutes. Next, add the cardamom pods and let it continue to boil until reduced to two thirds (around 15 minutes). Just before removing from heat, add the lemon juice and set aside to cool completely (30 to 45 minutes). Take the baklawa out of the oven and pour sugar syrup on top while still hot. Let the baklawa cool completely uncovered for around 30 minutes.

Garnish with ground walnuts or pistachios and rose petals (optional).

Notes

- *It is essential that when pouring sugar syrup on any dessert that the syrup is room temperature. If you pour hot syrup on a hot dessert, it will make it soggy and extra sweet in flavor. However, when it's room temperature, the dessert remains crunchy for several days with just the right amount of sweetness.*

- *A great hack: baklawa usually calls for brushing melted butter in between layers but if you have ever tried this method, you would know how hard it is to brush over a phyllo dough, due to how delicate and fragile those layers are. Therefore, I started using avocado spray instead. It's much easier, faster and gets the job done with the exact same results and taste.*

- *This is a double layered nut baklawa, meaning it has two layers of nuts. I've found that separating the nut mixture into two layers instead of one, prevents the nut mixture from becoming bulky and hard and provides a more airy and flaky texture to the overall baklawa.*

Almond Briouat

Almond briouat are sweet, crunchy, honey coated Moroccan triangle-shaped pastries stuffed with a sweet and nutty mixture of almond flour, sugar and traditionally—a hint of rose water. They are deep-fried to perfection then sprinkled with sesame seeds and drizzled with warm honey. They are eaten throughout the year and on special occasions and especially at teatime. I remember the first time I ever tried this dish when my Moroccan friend, Chef Asya, hosted a joint cooking class in Dubai back in 2011. My focus was teaching the students one Iraqi dish which was Parda Plau and Asya's was briouat. I was deeply mesmerized by how small and cute they were and how crunchy and delicious at the same time. I will always remember that day as the day I learned my first Moroccan recipe.

Yield 15–20 Pieces

For the Filling

1 cup (150 g) raw almonds, blanched and skin removed, divided

½ cup (100 g) granulated sugar

¼ cup (50 g) unsalted butter, melted

1 tsp mastic powder from 2-3 Mastic pearls, (optional)

½ tsp ground cinnamon

1 tbsp (15 ml) rose water

½ tsp salt

For the Glue

2 tbsp (16 g) all-purpose flour

3 tbsp (45 ml) water

Heat a large skillet with ⅓ inch (8 mm) of oil. Take ½ cup (75 g) of the almonds and slightly deep-fry them until they are light to medium gold, around 4 minutes. Take them out and place them on a plate with a paper towel to absorb the extra oil. Take the fried half and add it to a food processor with the rest of the raw almonds. Process for up to 5 minutes then add the sugar and blend well until it forms into a dough, around 2 minutes. Transfer to a large bowl and add the butter, mastic, cinnamon, rose water, salt and mix well until well combined. Start forming 1-inch (2.5-cm) balls, approximately ¼ to ⅓ ounce (5 to 10 g) if you are planning to go with the cherry sized briouat, or 2-inch (5-cm), approximately ⅓ to ½ ounce (10 to 15 g) balls, for the slightly larger ones. Keep making the balls until you run out of dough. Set them aside on a baking tray.

Prepare the glue by whisking the flour and water in a small bowl until fully combined and set aside.

(continued)

Notes

- *The recipe calls for toasting or deep-frying at least half of the raw almonds as that gives it its color, taste and texture. However, you can omit that step if you like.*

- *Briouat uses warqa (feuilles de brick ["brick pastry"]) or basteela sheets, which are paper thin dough sheets used a lot in Moroccan and North African cuisine. It is used to wrap the almond stuffing for briouat, however I noticed that using a double layered phyllo sheet or even flour-based spring roll sheets will provide you with a similar result.*

Almond Briouat (continued)

For the Dough

8 oz (227g) phyllo dough, thawed

1 pint (480 ml) honey

¼ cup (40 g) sesame seeds, toasted

To start preparing the dough, cut the phyllo dough into 2 x 10-inch (5 x 25-cm) sheets (cherry size) or 3 x 10-inch (8 x 25-cm) sheets for larger ones. Take two sheets and cover the rest with a damp cloth so they don't dry out. Next, place one of the almond balls at the far end of the sheet and start folding by wrapping the dough to cover the filling, then going up right then left until it is fully folded into a nice triangle. This should take around five folds. Then, seal the edge by brushing it with glue, and gently press down. Place on a baking sheet while making sure they remain covered with a damp cloth, so they don't dry out. Repeat the process with the remaining phyllo dough.

Heat a large pot with 2 cups (480 ml) of vegetable oil. Once it reaches 375°F (190°C), add a small batch of the triangles. Let them cook gently while flipping and moving them around in the oil, around 2 to 3 minutes. Once they are golden brown, take them out and place them on a cooling rack to remove excess oil. Next, place the honey in a pot and warm until it starts to bubble. Transfer to a bowl, add the sesame seeds and start submerging the fried briouats in the hot honey for a few seconds (if you want them slightly sweet) or leave them in longer for extra sweetness. Once they are sweetened to your taste, take them out gently and place in a strainer on top of a bowl. Let it sit there to drain for 10 to 15 minutes then transfer to a deep serving dish.

Notes

- *To grind the mastic pearls, place them in a mortar and grind them with ¼ teaspoon of granulated sugar. The result will be a powder-based mixture.*

- *Make sure the honey stays warm and doesn't become cold while covering the briouat as it will result in a very thick and gooey layer around them.*

- *Briouats can be stored in an airtight container and kept in the fridge for up to 1 week.*

Warbat Bil Qishta

This is a crunchy, buttery Arabic sweet made with several folded layers of phyllo dough, then stuffed to the brim with homemade qishta *and a drizzle of simple sugar syrup and garnished with crushed pistachios. Think of it like baklawa minus the nut stuffing and instead there is a layer of thick clotted cream. It is mostly popular throughout the month of Ramadan. I started making them at home a few years ago after I wanted to make an easier, lighter version of baklawa. You simply cannot go wrong with warbat.*

Yield 24 Pieces

For the Qishta

1 cup (240 ml) heavy cream

½ cup (120 ml) whole milk

2 tbsp (30 g) granulated sugar

1 tsp rose water or vanilla (optional)

¼ cup (30 g) all-purpose flour

5 tbsp (40 g) cornstarch

1 tsp orange blossom, optional

For the Simple Sugar Syrup

2 cups (400 g) granulated sugar

1 cup (240 ml) water

2-3 cardamom pods

½ lemon, juiced

For the Warbat

1 (16-oz [454-g]) package phyllo dough, thawed

1 cup (230 g) unsalted butter, melted

1¼ cups (150 g) crushed raw, unsalted pistachios

To make the qishta, in a medium-sized saucepan, add heavy cream, milk, sugar, vanilla (if you are using), flour and cornstarch and whisk well until they are fully absorbed and there are no lumps in sight. Place over medium heat and continue whisking periodically until it starts to thicken, around 5 minutes. Add the orange blossom and remove from the heat, then transfer to a bowl. Let it cool down completely then cover with plastic wrap, making sure the wrap touches the face of the cream entirely, to prevent hard skin from forming. Refrigerate for 2 hours.

For the simple sugar syrup, add the sugar and water to a saucepan over medium heat and let it boil for 3 to 5 minutes. Add the cardamom and lemon juice and let it boil over medium heat for 7 to 10 minutes, or until it becomes slightly thicker. Remove from the heat and let it cool down completely.

Preheat the oven to 375°F (190°C).

To prepare the dough, remove the phyllo dough from the wrap and place it under a damp cloth to prevent it from drying out. Take eight sheets of the dough and place them one on top of the other evenly on a working bench. Cut the stack of sheets in half. Take one half and place it back under the damp towel. Take the other half and cut into six equal squares around 5 x 5 inches (13 x 13 cm). Take each square and fold it into a triangle. Place the triangles on an oiled baking sheet, then drench them with the melted butter. Bake for 15 to 17 minutes or until golden and crispy. When they are done, take them out then drizzle the sugar syrup onto the hot baked dough. Let them cool completely for 3 to 5 minutes before stuffing them with the qishta (so the qishta maintains its texture and doesn't become runny). Add the qishta to a piping bag with an 807 round tip (can also be used without a tip). Open the triangle slightly and pipe in at least 3 tablespoons (45 g) of the qishta, then dip the raw edges into a bowl of crushed pistachios. Repeat the process with the remaining pastries.

Asawir Il Sit

If you love baklawa, then you are going to love these Nutella® stuffed bracelets. They are super delicate, crunchy and sweet. I remember years ago looking at them and thinking how hard it would be to make them, but they are much easier than you think. Using a single chopstick to roll the phyllo dough then scrunching it from both sides is all you need to do to create these masterpieces. And you can fill them with fresh pastry cream or Qishta instead of chocolate if you want.

Yield 25–30 Bracelets

For the Simple Sugar Syrup

1 cup (100 g) granulated sugar

½ cup (120 ml) water

Squeeze of lemon

For the Baklawa Bracelets

⅓ cup (75 g) clarified butter or ghee, melted

8 oz (227 g) phyllo dough, thawed

To make the sugar syrup, add the sugar and water to a pot and let boil until it has been reduced by ⅓, around 12 to 15 minutes. Add a squeeze of fresh lemon juice, then remove and let it cool down completely. Set aside.

Preheat the oven to 350°F (160°C). Prepare a baking sheet by brushing some clarified butter on it and set aside.

To make the baklawa bracelets, remove the phyllo dough from the package (cover with towel when not using, to prevent them from drying out). Using a knife, cut phyllo sheets into 7 x 6-inch (18 x 15-cm) size sheets. Take two sheets and cover the rest.

(continued)

Asawir Il Sit (continued)

For Garnishing

½ cup (140 g) Nutella

¼ cup (30 g) ground pistachios

Take a chopstick and place it horizontal to the 7-inch (18-cm) edge that is nearest to you. Start rolling towards the opposite side of you until you reach the last ¾-inch (2-cm) remaining of the dough. Push the rolled dough that is already around the chop stick from both sides inwards to create a scrunchy looking roll. Remove the stick then bring the edges together until you have a circular shaped piece then press the edges firmly on top of one another. Place in the buttered oven sheet and repeat the same process with the remainder of the dough. Drizzle melted butter on all the bracelets, and bake until crisp and golden brown, around 25 to 28 minutes. Once baked, pour the sugar syrup on top of the bracelets then add ½ tablespoon (10 g) Nutella in the middle of each one, sprinkle ground pistachios on top and serve with warm tea.

Notes

- *When rolling two sheets one on top of the other, you do not need to add butter in between, as they are easily rolled without it.*

- *You can choose to roll one sheet at a time; however, they will be very small and a bit delicate to handle.*

- *To make sure the bracelet edges stay stuck together, make a glue mixture of 2 tablespoons (16 g) flour and 3 to 4 tablespoons (45 to 60 ml) water. Mix well then dab your finger in it and brush the edges before sealing them.*

- *Authentic asawir il sit uses qishta (thick clotted cream) on top, that would be an option too if you are not a fan of Nutella or you can use melted chocolate instead.*

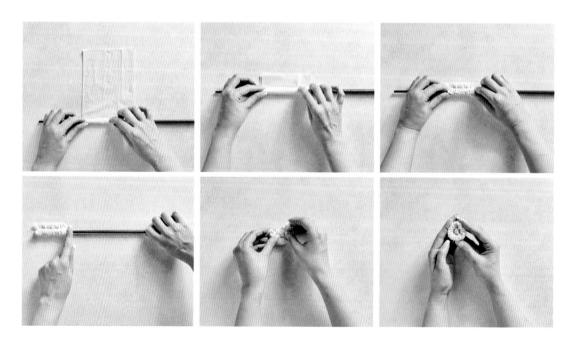

Zinood Il Sit

Crispy rolled phyllo dough, stuffed with clotted cream (qishta) is hands down, my all-time favorite dessert. I grew up eating them A LOT, and it was the one dessert that my mum would buy for me whenever I got good grades, did something good or just for the sake of spoiling me. She would go to a local dessert store that was at the end of our street. It was one of the most famous ones in the whole city called Ali Al Hamdani or "zinood il sit al hamdani" as most people called it. You would order by weight, so one kilo, two kilos or more! And you get to witness the beauty of those large silver pans being taken out of the oven and drizzled heavily with sugar syrup and a lot of fresh ground pistachios. What always makes them exceptionally good is the qishta filling and that was what made it different from the rest. They would place the pieces in a square box and stack it two rows high. I would love eating the ones at the top as they were less sugary, since all the excess sugar would soak through to the bottom pieces. I always thought the name was a bit weird. It translates to "the upper arm of a woman" referencing how the shape of the dessert looked like that part. As I said weird, but I like to think of it as an appreciation and celebration of the female body. Since I have not been able to go back home for more than 20 years now, I needed to find a way to recreate my favorite childhood dessert so imagine my joy when I found out just how easy they were to make at home . . . minus the extra sugar. You can choose to deep-fry them in vegetable oil or bake them in the oven.

Yield 20–24 Pieces

For the Qishta Filling

1 cup (240 ml) heavy cream

½ cup (120 ml) whole milk

3 tbsp (24 g) cornstarch

3 tbsp (45 g) granulated sugar

2 tsp (10 ml) rose water (optional)

1 tbsp (15 ml) orange blossom water (optional)

For the Simple Sugar Syrup

1 cup (200 g) granulated sugar

½ cup (120 ml) water

2 cardamom pods (optional)

1 tsp lemon juice

To make the filling, in a medium saucepan, add heavy cream, milk, cornstarch and sugar and whisk well until it is fully dissolved. Place over medium heat and continue whisking slowly for up to a minute until it starts to bubble. It will gradually thicken. Once it does, add in the rose water and orange blossom (if using). Remove the pan from the heat, transfer to a bowl and let it cool completely. Cover it with plastic wrap, making sure the wrap touches the face of the cream entirely. (This is to prevent a hard skin from forming). Place in the fridge for 1 hour. The filling is good for at least 4 days covered in the refrigerator.

For the sugar syrup, in a medium saucepan, add sugar and water and place over medium heat. Once it reaches a boil, add the cardamom (if using) and lemon juice. Let it continue boiling for another 5 to 7 minutes until it thickens slightly. Then remove from stove and let it cool completely.

(continued)

Zinood Il Sit (continued)

For the Glue

1 tbsp (8 g) all-purpose flour

3 tbsp (45 ml) water

For the Zinood

8 oz (227 g) phyllo dough, thawed

½ cup (125 g) qishta (optional)

Vegetable oil, for deep frying

For Garnishing

½ cup (75 g) ground pistachios

Prepare the glue. In a small bowl, mix the flour with the water until it forms into a thick liquid consistency, set aside.

For the zinood, take the phyllo dough out of its wrap and place under a damp cloth so it doesn't dry out. Take all the sheets of the dough and cut lengthwise into two to three equal sized pieces, around 5 to 6 inches (12 to 15 cm). Take two of those pieces and place the remaining ones back under the damp cloth. On a flat working surface, lay the sheets flat. Take the filling out from the fridge and place in a stand mixer. Add the qishta and whisk well for up to 2 minutes. Omit this step if you do not plan on using the qishta; just take the filling out from the fridge and whisk by hand before using. Take 2 table-spoons (30 g) of filling and add to the bottom part, ½ inch (1.25 cm) away from the edge. Fold both sides inwards, then start wrapping it firmly but gently like you would with a spring roll from the qishta side and continue rolling until it has been fully rolled. Brush a bit of the glue at the last ½ inch (1.25 cm) to make sure it is sealed and stays sealed. The size should be around 4 inches (10 cm) in length. Place it on a baking sheet lined with parchment paper, cover it with a cloth and repeat the process until all pieces have been fully wrapped. Place the tray in the freezer for 30 minutes to set.

While they are still in the freezer, fill a pot about ⅔ of the way with vegetable oil, making sure there is enough oil to cover the zinood. Let the oil reach 350°F (180°C). Once the oil is to temperature, take the zinood out of the freezer. Deep-fry two to three pieces at a time to maintain the temperature of the oil and let them cook for 1 to 2 minutes on each side or until golden. Take them out of the oil and dip directly into the sugar syrup. Dunk completely for 5 to 10 seconds if you like the sugar light or for 30 seconds if you like it sweeter. Once they are soaked, take them out and place them on a rack to remove excess syrup. Sprinkle pistachios on top or on both sides and serve.

Notes

- *You can freeze extra uncooked zinood fingers by placing them in an airtight bag. They are good for up to 2 months.*

- *If you feel like baking them instead, preheat the oven to 350°F (220°C). Place the rolls onto a baking sheet with parchment paper. Gently brush melted butter on each one of them, then bake for 25 to 28 minutes or until golden. Some of them might burst slightly but that is normal. Take them out then dip into sugar syrup for 10 seconds. Place them on a wire rack before placing them on a serving dish. Sprinkle ground pistachios on top and serve immediately if you like them extra crispy.*

Phyllo Cigars

I've been enjoying creating baklawa recipes more than I like to admit; there's just something about phyllo pastry that makes me want to eat it all the time. That crunchy dough, once baked, is remarkably delicious and works so well with other ingredients. This recipe is simple but very satisfying. It's slightly longer and slimmer, stuffed with nuts, dipped in melted chocolate and has the best crunch ever. They are a delight and a crowd pleaser for sure. You can freeze them before deep-frying (or baking if you want to go light) and just cover them in chocolate before serving, as simple as that!

Yield 22–25 Pieces

For the Cigars

8 oz (227 g) phyllo dough, thawed

1 cup (125 g) ground pistachios, divided

¼ cup (60 g) butter, melted

For the Simple Sugar Syrup

2 cups (400 g) granulated sugar

1 cup (240 ml) water

2–3 cardamom pods

½ lemon, juiced

For Frying

Canola oil for deep frying

For Garnishing

1½ cups (300 g) 70% dark chocolate

¼ cup (30 g) ground pistachios

¼ cup (30 g) ground walnuts

Once the phyllo dough has been fully thawed, remove it from the package and cover completely with a slightly damp towel. (Phyllo dough tends to harden quickly). Cut each phyllo sheet into three equal pieces. Place one piece on a flat surface, covering the rest with the towel. Add 1 tablespoon (7 g) of ground pistachios near one of the edges, making sure you leave about 1 inch (2.5 cm) from the edge. Brush melted butter on all edges and fold the left and right side of the dough. Butter the new edges and start rolling from the pistachio edge until fully rolled. Place on a flat oven sheet, cover with damp towel and repeat with remaining pieces of dough. Place the sheet, covered with plastic wrap, in the freezer, for at least 30 minutes. Take it out before frying.

Prepare the sugar syrup by adding the sugar, water and cardamom to a medium-sized pot. Boil over medium heat for 10 to 12 minutes or until a third of the quantity has been reduced. Add the squeeze of fresh lemon and set it aside.

Add canola oil to a deep pan and place over low to medium heat. Take the cigars out of the freezer. Once the oil is hot, around 375°F (190°C), add one roll at a time, making sure you don't dump them all in at once as that will lower the temperature of the oil and this will cause them to turn soggy. Fry 3 to 4 pieces at a time. Deep-fry for at least 1 minute on each side or until golden. Take them out and place on a rack. Drizzle the sugar syrup immediately over top. Melt the chocolate in a bowl using a microwave or a double boiler. Then dip one end of the roll in the chocolate. While still melted, sprinkle ground pistachios or walnuts on the chocolate. Place in the fridge for 15 to 20 minutes to set. After 20 minutes, take them out and serve with Qahwa (page 169).

Muakaja

The word muakaja *means crinkled in Arabic. Originally from Iraq, it is one of the easiest and most delicious Middle Eastern desserts. It did take the internet by storm about a year ago, but it has been in our kitchens for years. I am quite glad that a lot of people are discovering it. It is basically phyllo dough that is soaked in custard and baked in the oven until crispy, then is either drizzled with sugar syrup (or not if you like it less sweet) and served hot or cold. I kind of liked it better the next day with a cup of hot black cardamom tea, as I felt the custard had really oozed into the phyllo dough and made it soft at the bottom but remained crunchy at the top.*

Yield 8–10 Servings

For the Simple Sugar Syrup

1 cup (200 g) granulated sugar

½ cup (120 ml) water

½ tsp ground cardamom

For the Dough

½ cup (115 g) butter, melted

1 (16-oz [454-g]) package phyllo dough, thawed

For the Custard

2 cups (480 ml) whole milk

½ cup (100 g) granulated sugar

4 eggs

1 tsp ground cinnamon

1 tsp vanilla extract

For Garnishing

½ cup (60 g) ground pistachios

Note *If you like it to be more custardy, add an additional 1 cup (240 ml) of milk, 1 cup (200 g) of sugar and 1 more egg to the mixture.*

Prepare the sugar syrup by adding the sugar, water and cardamom to a small saucepan. Let it boil for up to 10 minutes over medium heat while mixing occasionally. Once it's thickened, remove from heat and let it cool.

For the dough, preheat the oven to 400°F (205°C). Grease a 9 x 4-inch (22 x 10-cm) oven dish with melted butter. Open the phyllo package and spread the dough sheets on a flat surface. Take out one sheet at a time, while covering the rest with a damp towel so they do not dry out. Spread the sheet flat on a working bench and brush melted butter on top. Using both of your hands, hold the bottom corners with each hand and start gradually gathering the edges on each side, creating a crinkled dough in the process that looks like a Japanese folding fan. Hold the two full edges firmly, one in each hand and place it on one end of the greased oven dish. Repeat the process until all phyllo sheets are in the dish. Place in the oven for 15 minutes then take it out.

While the phyllo is being baked, start working on the custard. Add milk, sugar, eggs, cinnamon and vanilla to a heavy saucepan and let it gently cook while constantly whisking over medium to low heat for about 15 minutes or until it thickens. Once it has thickened, remove from heat and let it cool.

Once it has cooled, pour the custard on top of the phyllo pan then bake again for 15 to 20 minutes or until golden and crispy and the custard is cooked. Once it's done, take out and sprinkle the crushed pistachios on top. Cut into square pieces and serve with clotted cream or vanilla ice cream and a drizzle of sugar syrup.

Note *A package of phyllo dough contains around 16–18 sheets. You can choose to double the layers when crinkling them or crinkle the sheets one by one. However, if your oven dish is smaller then make sure you do not over stack as the custard will not be able to penetrate the sheets and it will remain on top of them.*

Burma

My love for Burma is so big. It's like a fancy version of baklawa. The ingredients are the same but instead of layering the ingredients like baklawa, it is rolled instead. The word Burma in Arabic means that "the subject has been rolled", and as the name suggests, it is rolled instead of layered. It tends to be richer in pistachio taste and slightly less crunchy than baklawa. I like it this way a bit more as it is crunchy from the outside but very soft and full of flavor on the inside.

Yield 20–25 Pieces

For the Dough

2⅓ cups (235 g) raw pistachios, chopped, plus more for garnish

¾ cup (150 g) granulated sugar

8 oz (227 g) phyllo dough, thawed

½ cup (115 g) butter, melted

For the Simple Sugar Syrup

1 cup (200 g) granulated sugar

½ cup (120 ml) water

½ tsp ground cardamom

Rose water (optional)

Preheat oven to 350°F (190°C) and grease a 9 x 13-inch (22 x 33-cm) baking sheet with butter then set aside.

In a large bowl, mix the pistachios and sugar together and set aside. Cut the phyllo pastry in half. Take three layers at a time while making sure the rest are covered with a slightly damp cloth to prevent them from drying. Place the three sheets on top of each other and butter the top one slightly. Start sprinkling the pistachio mix on top of the layers while making sure that you don't cover the upper and lower edges.

Prepare to roll the layers by placing a chopstick on the bottom edge and rolling the layers around it. Roll it up completely then push the left and right ends towards the center as if you're scrunching it. Once it looks scrunched, remove the chopstick gently and place the roll on the baking sheet. Repeat the process until you run out of dough. Cut each roll while on the baking sheet into three to four equal pieces. Drizzle more butter on top, place in the oven and bake for 40 to 45 minutes or until golden.

For the sugar syrup, in a medium saucepan over medium heat, add the sugar and water. Once it reaches a boil, add the cardamom and let it continue to boil for another 5 to 7 minutes, until it thickens slightly. Add the rose water (if using), then remove from the stove and let it come to room temperature.

While the rolls are still hot, pour the sugar syrup on top. Lastly, sprinkle with pistachios and serve with Qahwa (page 169).

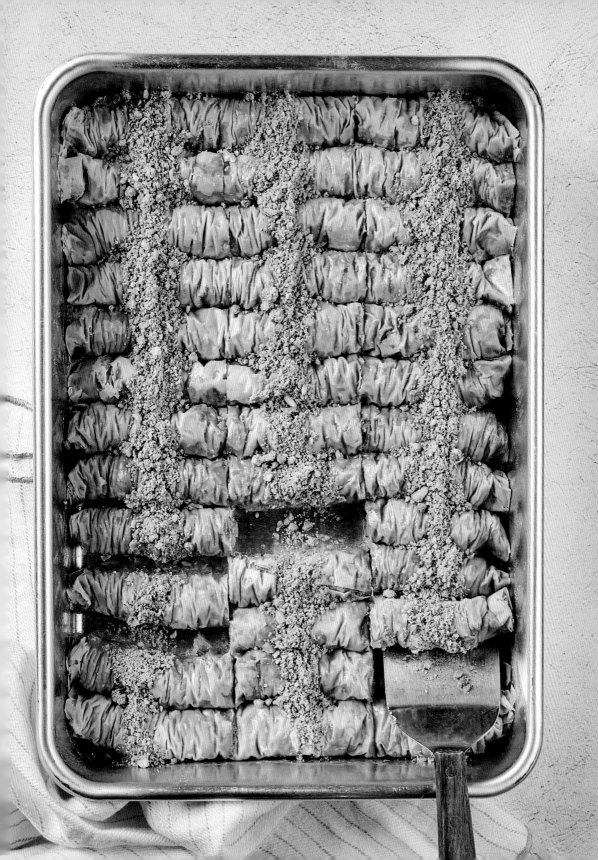

Baklawa Bites

Baklawa but in mini size? Sign me up! These baklawa bites are such a cool way of elevating your baklawa game to the next level. Individual bites are great for your next gathering and are so fun and easy to make.

Yield 20 Servings

For the Simple Sugar Syrup

1 cup (200 g) granulated sugar

½ cup (120 ml) water

2-3 cardamom pods, broken

For the Bites

8 oz (227 g) phyllo dough, thawed

1 cup (120 g) walnuts, finely chopped

1 cup (120 g) raw pistachios, finely chopped

¾ cup (200 g) unsalted butter, melted and divided

2 tsp (6 g) ground cinnamon

½ cup (100 g) granulated sugar

Melted chocolate, for garnish (optional)

Remove the phyllo dough from the package and cover it with a slightly damp cloth to prevent it from drying out.

To prepare the sugar syrup, place sugar, water and cardamom pods in a deep saucepan. Let it boil over medium heat for 15 minutes until it slightly thickens and set aside.

Preheat oven to 350°F (180°C).

To prepare the nut mixture, add the walnuts, pistachios, ½ cup (115 g) of the melted butter, cinnamon and sugar to a bowl and mix well then set aside. Place all phyllo sheets flat out on a working bench. Take one sheet and lay it flat, brush slightly with melted butter then place the second sheet on top and brush with butter. Repeat the process for all ten sheets. Using a knife, cut 4-inch (10-cm) square pieces.

Spray a muffin tin with oil spray, add the layers of cut dough in each one and press until the dough is touching the bottom of the tin. It is fine to have edges of the dough on the outside as it will give it a cup form and holds the nut mixture better. Repeat the process until the muffin tin is filled with the dough. Add 3 to 4 tablespoons (45 to 60 g) of nut mixture into each one. Place in the oven for 20 to 25 minutes or until golden. Take them out and drizzle with sugar syrup and melted chocolate (if using). Serve with Qahwa (page 169).

Kataifi Dreams

Kataifi pastry is one of my favorite types of dough. It is so versatile and can be used in savory and desserts alike. Here I'm sharing many ways of using it in a few delectable desserts. Some are traditional, others are more modern. I've learned throughout the years of using it in my dishes that whenever you find it to be a bit hard to use, you can simply spray it slightly with water then pop it in the microwave for 20 to 30 seconds. This will help in making it soft again. When it comes to fat, ghee is superior and works wonders with kataifi, however good quality butter is also a good option. As the melted ghee or butter saturates the dough, it ensures that it crisps and browns during the baking process—producing a fluffy, delicate pastry that melts in your mouth like Kunafa (page 113) or Kunafa Rolls (page 117).

Kunafa

Kunafa or Knafeh is made from kataifi *which is a shredded, thin noodle-like phyllo dough that is layered on a pan then stuffed with soft cheese such as sweet cheese,* nabulsi *or mozzarella. It's soft from the inside but crunchy from the outside and filled with flavor. My first time trying it was in Amman, Jordan while I was visiting the country for two weeks during Ramadan. The kunafa was orange in color as they use a special food coloring. It was stuffed with nabulsi cheese (which is quite salty but had been soaked a day before to remove the saltiness) then drizzled with ghee and baked until golden. It was then heavily drizzled with sugar syrup and some ground pistachios. This was the moment I fell in love with kunafa—after that first bite everything changed. My kunafa is not a nabulsi based one as the cheese is hard to find, but instead my very own version of a delicious kunafa that is simply irresistible.*

Yield 8–10 Servings

For the Simple Sugar Syrup

2 cups (400 g) granulated sugar

1 cup (240 ml) water

3-4 cardamom pods

½ lemon, juiced

For the Dough

1 (16-oz [454-g]) package kataifi dough, thawed

1 cup (225 g) ghee or butter, melted

5½ cups (600 g) low moisture mozzarella cheese

Note *For a different variety, you can add 1 cup (240 ml) Qishta (page 14) or heavy cream with the mozzarella to give the kunafa a creamy-like center.*

To prepare the syrup, add the sugar, water and cardamom pods to a pot and let it boil for up to 10 minutes over medium to high heat. Once it has thickened slightly, add the lemon juice and remove it from the heat. Let it cool completely.

Preheat oven to 350°F (190°C).

To begin preparing the dough, place the dough into a microwave for 30 seconds so it becomes soft. You can also spray it with water a couple of times to make it soft and easier to handle. Place the softened dough on a large cutting board, and with a knife, slice it into very small pieces. You can also use a food processor by adding the dough, then pulse four to five times until it is finely shredded but not too fine that it becomes like flour. Once the dough is finely shredded, add the dough to a large bowl. Pour in the melted butter and mix until all the dough has been fully covered by the butter.

Prepare a 12-inch (30-cm) round oven pan by brushing melted butter until the pan is fully covered. Add two-thirds of the mixture and spread evenly. Shred the cheese with your fingers and spread a thick layer on top of the dough. Cover the cheese with the remainder of the dough, making sure that the cheese is not visible and fully covered. Place the pan in the oven and bake for 40 to 50 minutes or until golden. Take it out and pour the sugar syrup on top. (Make sure the syrup is at room temperature before pouring.) Let the kunafa cool down before slicing. Serve with ice cream, whipped cream or qishta.

Osmalieh

Osmalieh, also called rough kunafa *in Palestine and Jordan or* Bas'ma *in Tripoli, Lebanon, is a very refreshing dessert that looks like a giant sandwich made from baked Kataifi dough. The crust is stuffed with qishta or sweet cheese and drizzled with sugar and garnished with pistachios and orange blossom. It is crispy on the outside and delightfully soft and sweet on the inside. The difference between osmalieh and regular kunafa is that osmalieh doesn't require the dough to be shredded; that's why it is called "rough kunafa," referencing how much the dough has been shredded. It is just loosely placed and baked separately until golden then assembled after, whereas regular kunafa is mostly shredded kataifi dough and baked along with the filling all together in one oven dish.*

Yield 8 Servings

For the Simple Sugar Syrup

2 cups (400 g) granulated sugar

1 cup (120 ml) water

2-3 cardamom pods

1 tsp rose water (optional)

For the Qishta

2 cups (480 ml) heavy cream

1 cup (240 ml) whole milk

3 tbsp (60 g) cornstarch

2 tbsp (30 ml) sugar syrup or granulated sugar

1 tsp orange blossom water (optional)

1 tsp rose water (optional)

1¼ cups (150 g) raw pistachios, chopped

For the Dough

1 (16-oz [454-g]) package kataifi dough, thawed

1 cup (250 g) ghee or clarified butter, melted

Note *You can make the osmalieh a bit thicker like the picture by adding an additional package of kataifi dough and double the amount of ghee.*

To make the sugar syrup, add sugar, water and cardamom to a large saucepan. Let it boil for 12 to 15 minutes over medium heat. Once it has thickened slightly, add the rose water (if using) and remove from the heat to let it cool completely. Set aside.

To make the qishta layer, add the heavy cream, milk, cornstarch and sugar syrup in a medium-sized saucepan and whisk for 5 to 7 minutes over medium heat until it starts to thicken. Then add the orange blossom and rose water (if you are using them) and once the consistency is thick enough, remove from heat, transfer to a bowl and let it cool completely. Then cover it with plastic wrap, making sure it touches the face of the cream to prevent it from creating a hard surface. Place in the fridge for 1 to 2 hours.

Preheat the oven to 380°F (180°C).

To make the layers, prepare two 10-inch (25-cm) deep baking dishes by oiling them with butter or avocado oil spray. Set these aside. In a large bowl, add the dough. Separate it lightly as if you were separating two tangled strings from one another. Continue with all the dough then pour the melted ghee on top. Using your hands, rub the ghee in well, then divide the mixture equally among the two baking dishes. Press gently but firmly to make sure it holds its shape (you can use the base of a ramekin to achieve that). Bake for 20 to 22 minutes or until golden. Take it out of the oven and pour sugar syrup on top while it's still hot. Let it sizzle then cool down before assembling the osmalieh.

To assemble the osmalieh, in a large serving dish place one of the baked kataifi layers. Next, take the qishta out and whisk gently to make it smooth and creamy, then spread on top of the first layer. Then add the second layer of the kataifi on top of the qishta. Lastly, sprinkle the pistachios and allow it to cool in the fridge for at least 2 hours. Slice it like you would a cake and serve with extra sugar syrup if required.

Kunafa Rolls

I'm just loving how versatile kataifi dough can be and I keep finding ways to recreate and make bite-sized variations. This recipe is a rolled kataifi dough that is stuffed with a cheesy cream mixture and baked till golden then drizzled with sugar syrup on top—making it a perfect delight for the afternoon.

Yield 20–25 Pieces

For the Filling

1 cup (240 ml) milk

1 cup (240 ml) heavy cream

¼ cup (30 g) cornstarch

3 tbsp (45 g) granulated sugar

A few drops of rose water (optional)

2 cups (225 g) mozzarella cheese

For the Kunafa

16 oz (454 g) kataifi dough, thawed

1 cup (250 g) ghee or clarified butter, melted

For the Sugar Syrup

2 cups (240 ml) granulated sugar

½ cup (120 ml) water

2–3 cardamom pods

1 tsp rose water (optional)

For Garnishing

½ cup (50 g) pistachios, chopped

Prepare a baking sheet with parchment paper and set aside.

To make the cream filling, place milk, heavy cream, cornstarch, sugar and rose water (if you are using) in a large pot over medium-low heat. As soon as it becomes thick, (around 7 to 9 minutes), remove from heat and add the cheese, mixing until fully melted. Set aside while it cools completely.

Preheat the oven to 380°F (195°C).

To make the rolls, spread out the soft dough on your work surface. Start by taking a few long strands from it, about 6-8 x 3-4 inches (15-20 x 8-10 cm). Brush a bit of melted butter on the dough and using your hands, start spreading the butter to evenly cover the strands. At the same time, take a different strand of dough about 3 x 4 inches (8 x 10 cm) and spread the butter evenly across it with your hands. Place the long strands on your working bench, with one end facing you. Then place the shorter one across the end that is facing you. Add 1 tablespoon (15 ml) of the qishta in the middle of the smaller piece. Then wrap its edges around it and start rolling the longer strand away from you until it is completely rolled.

Repeat for the reamining dough. Place the rolls on a baking sheet lined with parchment paper and bake for 20 to 22 minutes or until golden.

While the rolls are in the oven, make the sugar syrup. Add the sugar, water and cardamom pods to a pot over medium heat and mix until the sugar is completely dissolved. Continue boiling until it becomes thick. Then add the rose water (if using) and set aside to cool.

Once the rolls are done, add a drizzle of sugar syrup over them, sprinkle with pistachios and serve with Qahwa (page 169).

Extra Sweet

There's one thing that Arabic people excel in more than anything else and that is pouring sugar syrup on top of their desserts. It might be a weird concept in the beginning, but what differentiates Arabic sweets from Western sweets is that Arabic sweets have little to no sugar at all in their main ingredients. The sweetness comes entirely from the sugar syrup that is poured on top at the last step before serving. As a person who has a huge sweet tooth but doesn't like my sweets or desserts overly sweet, I appreciate this method a lot. This way, I get to enjoy making *Halawat Il Jibn* (page 134; one of my favorite desserts) while controlling the amount of sugar by adding just one spoonful of sugar syrup on top. (And if you like it sweeter then you can add more.) So for me, that is where the beauty of this method lies. And as much as I would like to think otherwise, I cannot say the same when it comes to store-bought Arabic sweets as they are bathed in sugar syrup. But that is why we are here making it at home, to our liking and desire and for the love of our dental and our blood sugar health.

Lukaimat

These delicious brown dumplings are deep-fried and smothered in date syrup or sugar syrup. A popular Arabian Gulf favorite– these sweet balls are crunchy, airy and soft all at the same time. The fried exterior is slightly hard, but when you break through, soft mush fills your mouth. This delicacy is normally made by Bedouin women in round deep pans. Thirty to fifty are made at any one time. It is even sometimes topped with Nutella®.

Yield 35-40 balls

For the Simple Sugar Syrup

2 cups (400 g) granulated sugar

1 cup (240 ml) water

2–3 cardamom pods

½ lemon, juiced

For the Dough

1 tbsp (10 g) active dry yeast

2 tbsp (30 g) granulated sugar

1¾ cups (420 ml) water, lukewarm (110°F [43°C]), divided

3 cups (375 g) all-purpose flour

Pinch of salt

For Deep Frying

6 cups (1.4 L) canola oil

To make the sugar syrup, mix sugar, water and cardamom in a pot over medium heat. Let it boil for 10 minutes. Once it is slightly thickened, add the lemon juice. Remove from heat and let it cool completely.

For the dough, mix yeast, sugar and 6 tablespoons (90 ml) of warm water in a small bowl. Let it proof for 10 minutes. In a larger bowl, add flour, salt and the yeast mixture. Mix well, then gradually add the remaining warm water while continuously whisking for up to 6 minutes until it reaches a very soft consistency. It should look a bit more watery than regular dough. Cover the dough with plastic wrap and a large warm cloth and let it rest for up to 2 hours.

Add oil to a deep pot and heat it to 365°F (185°C). Fill a frosting bag (no tip needed) with the dough mixture. Seal it tight from the top and start squeezing the dough out right on top of the pot filled with oil. Cut it every 1 inch (2.5 cm) to form small balls. Repeat the process until you use up all the dough. Make sure you flip the balls to the other side after 1 minute. Make sure all sides are golden brown before removing it from the oil. Then transfer the balls to a bowl lined with paper towels. After the excess oil has been absorbed, (about 5 minutes) add the balls to the sugar syrup then take them out after 20 seconds to avoid over-soaking them with sugar syrup. Serve immediately with Qahwa (page 169).

Zlabiya

One of my favorite memories in Baghdad was the food street vendors. There were certain places like Al Kadimia that were famous for their markets and street food. It was a heavily crowded area located around a famous mosque that people would eagerly visit for worship. The markets were just beside it and you could literally find anything and everything there—from clothes to fabrics to spices, nuts, kitchen utensils and cookware—and finally, the food street vendors. I remember they were usually located near the roundabouts just before you enter the market and right after you leave. They usually had a small cart filled with huge, round silver trays full of sweets like halwa, dihinia, Burma and zlabiya. Zlabiya, overall has a very distinctive texture and rich taste. It's crispy and slightly hollow inside with a burst of rich sugar syrup.

Yield 8 Servings

For the Simple Sugar Syrup

1 cup (240 ml) water

3 cups (600 g) granulated sugar

½ lemon, juiced

2 cups (480 ml) glucose syrup

For the Dough

2 cups (240 g) all-purpose flour

2½ cups (300 g) cornstarch

1 tsp salt

1 tsp baking soda

1 tsp baking powder

2½ cups (620 ml) water, lukewarm, divided

1 tbsp (10 g) active dry yeast

2 tsp (8 g) granulated sugar (optional)

For Deep-Frying

1 qt (960 ml) canola oil

To make the sugar syrup, in a large pot add the water and sugar. Place over medium heat and boil until the sugar is completely dissolved and starts to boil, around 7 minutes. Then add the lemon juice and let it boil for another 2 minutes. Lastly, add the glucose syrup and mix gently until fully combined which will take around 2 minutes. Remove the syrup from heat and set aside.

To prepare the dough, in a large bowl, mix the flour, cornstarch, salt baking soda and baking powder and set aside. In a small bowl, mix 1 cup (240 ml) of water with the yeast and sugar (if using) and let it proof for 10 minutes. Then add the rest of the water and the flour mixture. Mix well then cover with plastic wrap and a kitchen towel and let it rest for 1 hour. Uncover the bowl, whisking gently until you have a good batter.

Add the oil to a deep pan over medium heat, until it reaches 365°F (185°C). While the oil heats up, transfer the batter to a squeeze bottle with a ¼ inch (5 mm) tip or a ketchup squeeze bottle with a large opening (that can be done by cutting the tip with a scissors). Once the oil is hot, start squeezing the batter into the oil, forming a circular spiral-like shape in the oil. Cook for 30 seconds to 1 minute on each side or until golden. Make sure the syrup is warm then transfer the spirals to the syrup and dunk them until fully covered. Leave them submerged for 30 to 45 seconds then take them out and transfer to a bowl to serve.

Note *They are good for up to 2 days to maintain their crunchiness.*

Balah Al Sham

Balah Al sham which translates to "dates of Damascus" is considered one of the most famous and popular Middle Eastern desserts especially in Iraq and Syria. It is also popular in Turkey but there it is called tulumba. *The only difference is that it is soaked into a simple sugar syrup instead of dusted with cinnamon and powdered sugar. These delicious churro-like treats go by many different names depending on what country you are from.*

Yield 20–25 Pieces

For the Simple Sugar Syrup

1 cup (240 ml) water

3 cups (600 g) granulated sugar

3-4 cardamom pods

2½ cups (600 ml) glucose syrup (optional)

1 tsp rose water (optional)

For the Dough

1½ cups (188 g) all-purpose flour

Pinch of salt

¾ cup (170 g) butter, softened

2 cups (480 ml) water, boiling

6 eggs

For Deep Frying

4-6 cups (960-1440 ml) canola oil

To make the sugar syrup, add the water, sugar and cardamom into a small pot. Place it over medium heat and let it boil for 10 to 12 minutes until it thickens. Remove from the heat and add the glucose syrup and rose water (if using). Mix well and set aside.

To make the balah al sham, sift the flour into a large bowl and add a pinch of salt, then set aside. Place a pot on the stove over low heat. Then add the butter and water and let it simmer. Gradually add the flour while whisking to create a smooth dough consistency. Let it cook for up to 4 minutes on low heat while continuing to mix with a spatula until it forms a dough and starts to pull away from the pot. Remove from the heat and transfer to a stand mixer, letting it cool down slightly. Using the dough hook attachment, start mixing for 2 minutes then add the eggs one at a time while whisking until it forms a soft smooth dough, around 5 minutes. Prepare a piping bag with a 4B tip and add the dough to it.

Heat a large pot over medium heat and add the canola oil. While it is still warming up (oil should be warm not hot), start piping finger length pieces of dough into the oil. Cut the dough using clean scissors. Place six to eight at a time and increase the temperature to high. As soon as the fingers start to brown (around 3 to 5 minutes) flip it over to the other side to brown too, then remove it and place directly into the syrup filled pot. Dip each finger gently then remove immediately and place into a serving bowl. Repeat the process with the remaining dough and make sure to lower the temperature before adding the pieces and increasing it after.

Notes

- *Fingers can be kept at room temperature for 2 to 4 days.*
- *Glucose syrup provides a lovely, finished shine to the final product and maintains its crunchiness. However, you can omit it if you do not have it.*

Mafrouka

One of my favorite no-bake, truffle-like desserts is this Lebanese delicacy—mafrouka. The word translates to rubbed *in Arabic. This literally means the pistachios are rubbed well with semolina on the stove until it forms into a paste. This paste is what will be used as the shell for this dessert. They are then stuffed with homemade clotted cream and drizzled with simple sugar syrup (optional). You can also swap the clotted cream with whipped ricotta that is sweetened with sugar. Mafrouka is both creamy and nutty, and there are several ways of presenting it, but the most popular way is truffle balls. The second method is by spreading it evenly on a plate then topping it with the thick clotted cream and a drizzle of sugar syrup. Either way you choose to make it, this dessert will be your new showstopper at any of your gatherings.*

Yield 28–34 Balls

For the Qishta

1 cup (240 ml) heavy cream

½ cup (120 ml) whole milk

2 tbsp (30 g) granulated sugar

2 tbsp (16 g) all-purpose flour

5 tbsp (40 g) cornstarch

1 tsp rose water or vanilla extract (optional)

For the Mafrouka

1¼ cups (150 g) raw pistachios, unsalted

¼ cup (60 g) unsalted butter

1 cup (170 g) course semolina

⅔ cup (130 g) granulated sugar

1 cup (240 ml) water

1 tsp orange blossom water (optional)

To make the qishta, in a medium saucepan, add heavy cream, milk, sugar, flour and cornstarch and whisk well until fully dissolved and there are no lumps in sight. Add in the rose water or vanilla if you choose to use it. Place over medium heat and continue whisking slowly for up to a minute until it starts to bubble. It will gradually thicken. Once it does, remove the pan from heat and transfer to a bowl. Let it cool completely, then cover with plastic wrap, making sure the wrap touches the face of the cream entirely. (This is to prevent hard skin from forming). Place in the fridge for 2 to 3 hours, until it is completely cold and holds its shape. The qishta is good, covered for at least 4 days in the refrigerator.

For the mafrouka, place the pistachios in a food processor and pulse a few times to create a smooth ground nutty texture with no large pieces then set it aside. In a medium saucepan, add the butter and let it melt over medium heat. Then add the semolina and cook for about 90 seconds while stirring with a spatula. Add the sugar and mix until fully combined. (The texture will resemble fluffy bread-crumbs). Next, add water and let it cook while constantly stirring until it changes from liquid into a thicker paste (around 5 minutes). Then add the pistachios and the orange blossom water (if you are choosing to use it) and cook while stirring for another couple of minutes. The dough will become slightly stickier and shinier at this point. Remove from heat and let it cool completely.

(continued)

Mafrouka (continued)

For the Simple Sugar Syrup

1 cup (240 ml) water

3 cups (600 g) granulated sugar

3-4 cardamom pods

2½ cups (600 ml) glucose syrup (optional)

1 tsp rose water (optional)

For Garnishing

⅔ cup (75 g) ground pistachios

Line a baking sheet with parchment paper. Begin to shape the mafrouka by using an ice cream scooper sprayed with oil. Take a scoop of the mafrouka dough, then place it on the baking sheet. Continue scooping balls with the remainder of the dough. With your thumb, press gently on each one to form a hollow area where you can place the qishta. Take the qishta out from the fridge, scoop about 2 to 3 teaspoons (7 to 11 ml) of qishta and place it in the hollow area. Do this step quickly so the thick cream doesn't melt. Once you have placed your cream inside the ball, gather the dough around the qishta to seal it shut. It should form a complete ball. Place your mafrouka on the baking sheet and repeat the process until all the dough has been filled and shaped.

To make the simple sugar syrup, add the water, sugar and cardamom into a small pot. Place it over medium heat and let it boil for 10 to 12 minutes until it thickens. Remove it from the heat and add the glucose syrup and rose water (if using). Mix well and let it cool completely, then set aside.

To garnish, place ground pistachios in a bowl, then dunk and completely cover every ball with the ground pistachios. Place them back on the sheet and keep refrigerated until it is time to serve. Once you are ready to serve, drizzle with sugar syrup before serving (optional).

Notes

- *For easier shaping, you can use mini semi spherical silicone molds and add half the pistachio mixture to the bottom of the mold, then 1 to 2 tablespoons (15 to 30 ml) qishta, and finally top it with another layer of the pistachio dough to fully seal it.*

- *For a crunchier texture, you can cover the balls with crushed pistachios before placing them in the fridge to set.*

- *To store the mafrouka, add them to an airtight container and keep in the fridge for up to 5 days.*

Qatayif

Qatayif is one of the most popular Middle Eastern desserts served during Ramadan. They are stuffed pancakes that can be left half open or completely closed like a sweet dumpling. You make the pancake then partially fold and seal up to one half, forming a sort of cornucopia shape. Then you fill the opening with qishta (or cream) and nuts. You can make smaller ones too by pouring only half the quantity of the batter then sealing it halfway and stuffing it with qishta (or cream). These smaller ones are called qatayif asafiri *which translates to* small bird. *They are usually drizzled with honey sugar syrup or just regular sugar syrup.*

Yield 25–30 Pieces

For the Honey Sugar Syrup

4 cups (800 g) granulated sugar

2 cups (480 ml) water

⅓ cup (80 ml) honey

½ lemon, juiced

For the Qishta

1 cup (240 ml) milk

1 cup (240 ml) heavy cream

3 tbsp (45 g) cornstarch

2 tbsp (30 g) granulated sugar

1 tsp vanilla extract

To make the honey sugar syrup, add the sugar and water into a small pot over medium heat. Let it boil without moving it at all and as soon as it boils, you can add the honey and lemon juice. Mix gently and let it boil for 10 minutes. Set aside and place in the fridge to cool down completely.

To make the qishta, add the milk and heavy cream to a pot over medium to low heat. Then add the cornstarch, sugar and vanilla and whisk well until fully combined. Let it boil gently on medium heat until it starts to have a custard-like consistency, around 5 minutes. Once it has thickened, set it aside to cool completely. Then cover it with plastic wrap, making sure the plastic wrap touches the surface of the cream so it doesn't become hard. Then place in the fridge for 1 to 2 hours.

(continued)

Qatayif (continued)

For The Dough

2 cups (480 ml) water, lukewarm (110°F [43°C])

1 cup (240 ml) whole milk, lukewarm (110°F [43°C])

2 tbsp (30 ml) canola oil

1 tsp vanilla extract

2½ cups (315 g) all-purpose flour

⅔ cup (110 g) fine semolina

2 tbsp (30 g) granulated sugar

5 tbsp (45 g) powdered milk

1 tbsp (10 g) active dry yeast

1 tsp baking powder

Pinch of salt

For the Garnishing

⅔ cup (75g) ground pistachios

To make the qatayif dough, place water, milk, oil and vanilla in a food processor. Then add the flour, semolina, sugar, powdered milk, yeast, baking powder and salt. Process well on medium speed until fully combined, around 3 minutes. It should be the consistency of a thin crepe batter. Let it rest until it becomes bubbly around 15 to 20 minutes. Place a nonstick crepe pan over high heat. Do not grease the pan as it will mess up the dough. Once the pan has reached 350°F (180°C), reduce the heat to medium. Use a ¼-cup (60-ml) measuring cup to measure out the batter (you can use half that quantity for smaller qatayif). Ladle the batter into the hot pan to create a 3-inch (8-cm) circular shape. Make sure you do not add more than four at a time, so the pan's temperature doesn't go down. You do not need to flip the pancake. You only need to cook it on one side and let the second side gradually cook by itself. Let the pancake cook for 30 seconds to 1 minute or until the bottom is a unified golden color and the top begins to form tiny bubbles, isn't shiny anymore and is fully dried. Take the pancake out and place it on a kitchen towel. The bubbly side tends to be sticky so make sure it's facing up. Cover the qatayif with plastic wrap so they stay soft. Repeat with the remainder of the batter, then cover all the pancakes with plastic wrap so they don't dry out (if it dries you will not be able to pinch the edges). Once you are ready to stuff the qatayif, hold one pancake in the palm of your hand, and use the other hand to fold it halfway, but not more so you have an open cone shape. Pinch the edges together all the way until you reach the middle. It should stay closed. Set it aside and repeat the process for all the pancakes.

Take the qishta out of the fridge, whisk it gently with a hand whisk and place it in a piping bag with no tip. Next, start stuffing the qatayif with approximately 1 tablespoon (15 ml) of cream. Drizzle with honey syrup just before serving. Garnish with pistachios by dipping the open edge of the qatayif into the pistachios.

Notes

- *You can use the back of the ladle to smooth over the batter in a circular motion to create the perfect circular shape.*
- *Qatayif can be eaten without the syrup for a lighter and healthier version.*
- *Qatayif dough can be kept in the fridge for a week.*
- *You can omit the honey in the sugar syrup. Just use water and sugar for a simple sugar syrup.*

Stuffed Qatayif

As the name suggests, these are qatayif but completely stuffed and sealed. These are the "wonton" shaped version mentioned in the previous recipe. Once sealed, these are deep-fried until golden and crispy. They are then dunked into a sugar syrup just before serving.

Yield 25 pieces

For the Qatayif

25 Qatayif pieces (page 129)

2 cups (240 g) walnuts, chopped

½ cup (100 g) granulated sugar

1 tsp ground cinnamon

For the Honey Sugar Syrup

4 cups (800 g) granulated sugar

2 cups (480 ml) water

¼ cup (60 ml) honey

½ lemon, juiced

For Deep Frying

Canola oil

Once you have completed making your qatayif pancakes, make sure they are fully covered with plastic wrap to maintain freshness and to prevent them from drying out. When they are dry, they will not be able to close and seal. In a bowl, mix the walnuts, sugar and cinnamon until fully combined. Set the nut mixture aside.

Prepare the honey sugar syrup. Add the sugar and water into a small pot over medium heat. Let it boil without moving it at all and as soon as it boils, you can add the honey and lemon juice. Mix it gently and let it boil for 10 minutes. Set aside and place in the fridge to cool down completely.

Heat a large pot with oil to 350°F (180°C).

Add 1 tablespoon (15 g) of the walnut mixture in the center of the pancake. Fold the pancake over the mixture until you have a half-moon shape. Use your fingers to pinch the edge shut. Once you have sealed the pancake, place it back under the plastic wrap so they remain soft. Repeat this process until you finish all of the pancakes. Fry each stuffed qatayif for up to 2 minutes on each side or until golden and crispy.

Have your bowl full of honey sugar syrup ready and as soon as the qatayif are fully golden, dunk them instantly into the syrup. If you don't like it too sweet then remove it after a couple of seconds. However, if you like it a bit sweeter then submerge it for a few seconds more. Remove them from the syrup and place them on a rack to drain excess syrup. Serve immediately with Qahwa (page 169).

Halawat Il Jibn

This is one of those Middle Eastern desserts that has a "wow" factor to it; whether it's the presentation or the taste. Halawat il jibn means "sweetness of cheese." It is a very interesting dessert from Lebanon. It's gooey, slightly chewy, very cheesy and looks like a Swiss roll but instead of a cake, it is a cheese paste. This paste is made from cheese and semolina, then stuffed with qishta, rolled and drizzled with sugar syrup and garnished with nuts to give it a slight crunch.

Yield 20 Pieces

For the Qishta

1 cup (240 ml) heavy cream

½ cup (120 ml) whole milk

2 tbsp (30 g) granulated sugar

5 tbsp (60 g) cornstarch

1 tsp rose water or vanilla
extract (optional)

For the Simple Sugar Syrup

2 cups (400 g) sugar

1 cup (240 ml) water

2–3 cardamom pods

½ lemon, juiced

For the Cheese Mixture

1½ cups (360 ml) water

1 cup (200 g) granulated sugar

1 tsp orange blossom water
(optional)

1 cup (167 g) fine semolina

4 cups (450 g) mozzarella
cheese, shredded

For Garnishing

¼ cup (60 g) ground pistachios

For the qishta, in a medium saucepan, add heavy cream, milk, sugar, cornstarch and rose water or vanilla (if you are using). Whisk well until everything is fully dissolved and there are no lumps in sight. Place over medium heat and continue whisking slowly for 3 to 5 minutes until it starts to bubble first then starts to gradually thicken. Remove from heat and transfer to a bowl. Let it cool down completely, then cover with plastic wrap, making sure the wrap touches the face of the cream entirely. This is to prevent hard skin from forming. Place in the fridge for 1 to 2 hours, or until completely cold and holds its shape. The qishta is good covered for at least 4 days in the refrigerator.

To make the sugar syrup place the sugar, water, cardamom and lemon juice in a pot over medium heat. Let it boil for 10 minutes, remove from heat and let it cool completely.

For the cheese mixture, heat the water in a large pot over medium heat. Add the sugar and orange blossom water if you are planning on adding it and let it dissolve completely. Then lower the heat and add the semolina and stir until the mixture thickens, around 4 minutes. Gradually add the cheese while stirring until all the cheese has melted. At this point, it will resemble thick porridge. Continue mixing until the dough has come together. Remove from the heat and let it cool down for 2 minutes. Separate the dough into 2 to 3 balls and then take one out and place it on a working bench covered with plastic wrap (edges tucked underneath the board). With a slightly oiled rolling pin, start gently rolling out the dough until it is ½ inch (2 cm) thick and measures 6 x 18 inches (15 x 45 cm).

Take the qishta out of the fridge and fill a piping bag with the cream. Squeeze out the qishta, forming a line of cream from one end of the cheese dough to the other end about 1 inch (2.5 cm) from the edge. Roll the dough over the qishta forming a log, making sure all the cream is contained inside. You can either roll it once or twice for a thicker roll. Cut the extra dough off and return it back to the bowl.

Take the edges of the plastic wrap out from underneath the board and start wrapping it around the roll, making sure to twist the ends like a Christmas cracker. Place the wrapped roll on a baking sheet and repeat the process for the remainder of the dough then place the baking sheet in the fridge for at least 2 hours, or until nice and firm. When it has firmed up, take it out of the fridge, remove the wrap and slice it into 2-inch (5-cm) slices. Brush the top of the slices with the sugar syrup to give it a shine and sprinkle the pistachios on top. Finish by drizzling more sugar syrup on top and serve with Chai Aswad (page 165).

Halwa

The word halwa *comes from the Arabic word* huluw, *which means sweet. However, the recipe can vary greatly from region to region and country to country. Typically, there are two types of halwa. One is made from tahini paste and the other is made from flour. The one that is most popular in the Middle East and that I grew up eating is the tahini based one. I remember going with my mum to local market areas in Baghdad. The markets were not merely a shop or two but instead very large areas with several buildings, streets and open grounds for the local vendors to sell easily to customers. Some of these street vendors would be selling food—especially sweets in very large round shaped stainless steel trays filled with halwa at the entrance of several market roads. I can still remember the aroma and delicious smell of it along with its flaky texture that melts in your mouth and that you can easily pick apart with just your fingers. What makes Halwa so good is the simplicity of its ingredients. Halwa can be eaten in many ways, whether by itself or spread on a piece of toast for breakfast. It is traditionally served with Qahwa (page 169) or Chai Bi Heil (page 166).*

Yield 8–10 Servings

1¼ cups (160 g) powdered sugar

1¼ cups (160 g) powdered milk

Pinch of salt

1 tsp vanilla powder

2 cups (400 g) tahini paste

½ cup (60 g) toasted pistachios, crushed

In a large bowl, sift the powdered sugar and the powdered milk (to prevent any lumps). Next, add the salt and vanilla powder and mix well and set aside. In a small pot, warm the tahini over low heat until it reaches 120°F (48°C), then add it gradually to the bowl of sugar and milk mixture while constantly stirring. At this point, you can add half of the pistachios if you like to have it inside your halwa. Mix everything together using your hands. At first, it will look like breadcrumbs but then it will gradually hold together a bit more until you can easily press on it with your hand, and it will hold its shape— around 6 to 8 minutes. This is the texture you want.

Grease and line a 9 x 4-inch (22 x 10-cm) loaf pan (or a smaller pan in any shape) with butter and parchment paper. Sprinkle the remaining pistachios at the bottom, then pour in the mixture and spread it evenly. Add another piece of parchment paper on top of the halwa and using another smaller pan, press firmly on the mixture to remove all the air from it. The firmer it is, the better the results. Place it in the refrigerator for at least 3 to 6 hours, up to 2 days to fully set. The end result is a flaky texture that melts in your mouth. To serve, slice and serve with Chai Bi Heil (page 166) or Qahwa (page 169).

Note *Halwa can be kept in an airtight container in the fridge for up to 4 to 6 months.*

Puddings and Soft Delights

Middle Eastern puddings are a favorite and enjoyed throughout the year. They are generally smooth, silky and creamy in texture, and can be served hot, like Sahlab (page 149) and Umm Ali (page 141), or cold, like Ishtaliah (page 142) or Leyali Lebnan (page 145). They are also flavored with a variety of ingredients like orange blossom, rose water, nuts and so much more.

Umm Ali

Umm Ali is an Arabic bread pudding variation that is somewhere between bread pudding and baklawa (page 89). What's wonderful about this Egyptian dessert is the heavenly combination between the delicious nuts and the creamy bread pudding which can be eaten hot or cold. For me personally, I love eating them both ways—when it's hot, it gives you that warm, nutty and creamy flavor and when it's cold, it gives you the strong texture of the pastry. You can also choose to have it with a lot of cream (or milk) or choose to go with it being a bit thicker in texture. Both are great so do try to prepare them both ways.

Yield 6 Servings

For the Pastry

1 (17-oz [490-g]) package puff pastry or (400 g) buttered croissant

⅔ cup (75 g) pistachios

¼ cup (25 g) sliced almonds

¼ cup (35 g) pine nuts

¼ cup (28 g) blanched almonds

¼ cup (60 ml) orange blossom water (optional)

¼ cup (35 g) raisins

For the Milk Mixture

½ cup (100 g) granulated sugar

4 cups (960 ml) milk

1 cup (240 ml) heavy cream, divided

1 tsp ground cardamom (optional)

2 tbsp (16 g) ground cinnamon

For Garnishing

3-4 tbsp (21-30 g) ground pistachios (optional)

Preheat the oven to 350°F (180°C).

Take the dough out of the freezer 1 hour in advance to allow it to defrost. In a small bowl, soak pistachios, almonds and pine nuts in the orange blossom water (if you are choosing to use it) for up to 30 minutes. Strain the nuts and set aside, discarding the orange blossom water. Spread the dough on a floured surface and using a rolling pin, gently roll until it is around inch (3 mm) thick. Cut it into three or four pieces (it doesn't really matter as we will be breaking it into pieces once baked). Place the dough on an oiled baking sheet and place it in the middle rack of the oven. Bake for 10 to 15 minutes until it's golden brown. Once it's done, take it out and let it cool. Once it has cooled, cut the larger pieces into small pieces with a knife or use your fingers and set aside.

Prepare the milk mixture by placing the sugar, milk, half the heavy cream, cardamom (if using) and cinnamon in a deep pot over medium heat and let the spices steep into the milk. Continue to simmer gently, around 5 to 7 minutes. At this point you can choose to add the remaining cream to it right now or choose to add it later drizzled on top. Remove from heat and set aside.

In a 9 x 4-inch (22 x 10-cm) baking dish, place half of the baked pastry as a first layer. Next, add a layer of the nut mixture and raisins. Then add the other half of the pastry on top of the nut mixture. Now slowly pour the milk mixture on top until fully covered. Let it rest for up to 10 minutes to allow the pastry to absorb the milk. If after this time, you still see that it needs more milk, add a bit more. If you have not added the cream to the milk mixture, then you can add it now as the top layer of the pastry. Place it in the oven and let it bake for 20 minutes, then place under the broiler for 5 minutes to give it a beautiful golden color. When it's nice and golden brown, take it out of the oven, sprinkle ground pistachios on top and the remainder of the cream if you chose not to add it to the milk mixture. Serve either hot or cold.

Ishtaliah

Ishtaliah derives from the word ashta *or* qishta *and means "cream pudding." It is a delicious Lebanese pudding that is slightly like panna cotta and is so simple and easy to make. It has a drizzle of simple sugar syrup and crushed pistachios on top to create the perfect dessert. I love the smoothness of the texture; it really does feel like you are indeed eating a cream pudding.*

Yield 4 Servings

For the Ishtaliah

3 cups (720 ml) whole milk

1 cup (240 ml) heavy cream

⅓ cup (50 g) cornstarch

¼ cup (50 g) granulated sugar, divided

3-4 mastic granules

½ cup (118 g) cream cheese

2-3 tbsp orange blossom water (optional)

1 tbsp rose water (optional)

For Garnishing

Handful of chopped pistachios

Fig slices

Honeycomb

2 cups (440 ml) simple sugar syrup (page 20), optional

Place a medium-sized saucepan over medium-low heat. Add the milk, cream, cornstarch and all but 1 teaspoon of the sugar to the pan. In a mortar, add the mastic and remaining sugar and grind into a powder, then add it to the milk mixture along with the cream cheese. Whisk gently on medium heat until the mixture starts to thicken, around 7 to 10 minutes. Add the orange blossom and rose water (if using), and mix gently to incorporate. Remove from heat and let it cool down. The result should be of thick, creamy consistency.

Transfer mixture to four 4-inch (10-cm) serving bowls. Place around 5 ounces (150 g) in each bowl. Cover with plastic wrap and place the bowls in the fridge to set for 6 hours. Once they are ready, take them out and flip each one on a plate like you would do with a panna cotta. Sprinkle pistachios on top, add figs and honeycomb and drizzle with sugar syrup (optional) before serving. Ishtaliah can be served with Qahwa (page 169) or Karak Chai (page 168).

Note *Mastic is a compound that is used heavily in Middle Eastern cuisine as a thickening agent. If you can't find it, you can use ⅓ cup (50 g) of cornstarch and mix with some milk separately to avoid lumps.*

Leyali Lebnan

Layali lebnan, meaning Lebanese nights, *is a delicious three-layered cold Lebanese semolina pudding that is traditionally flavored with orange blossom or rose water. It has a sponge-like texture to it and is covered with a good layer of qishta, a generous sprinkle of crushed pistachios (or any kind of fresh cut fruits like berries or bananas) then a drizzle of sweet sugar syrup. I love layali lebnan for its simplicity and its very rich taste that can please anyone with a sweet tooth. It can be stored for up to 5 to 6 days covered and sealed in an airtight container in the fridge.*

Yield 8 Servings

For the Qishta

1 cup (240 ml) heavy cream

½ cup (120 ml) whole milk

2 tbsp (30 g) granulated sugar

5 tbsp (60 g) cornstarch

1 tsp rose water or vanilla extract (optional)

For the Simple Sugar Syrup

2 cups (400 g) sugar

1 cup (240 ml) water

2-3 cardamom pods

½ lemon, juiced

For Leyali Lebnan

6 cups (1.4 L) whole milk

1 cup (170 g) course semolina

½ cup (100 g) muscovado sugar or granulated sugar

½ cup (60 g) cornstarch

2 tbsp (30 ml) orange blossom water or rose water

1 cup (185 g) toasted pistachios, crushed, for garnish

To prepare the qishta, in a medium saucepan, add the heavy cream, milk, sugar, cornstarch and rose water or vanilla (if you are using). Whisk well until everything is fully dissolved and there are no lumps in sight. Place over medium heat and continue whisking slowly for up to 7 minutes, until it starts to bubble first then starts to gradually thicken. Remove from heat and transfer to a bowl. Let it cool completely then cover with plastic wrap, making sure the wrap touches the face of the cream completely to prevent hard skin from forming. Place in the fridge for at least 2 hours until completely cold and holds it shape.

To make the sugar syrup, place the sugar, water and cardamom in a pot over medium heat. Let it boil for 10 minutes, add the lemon, boil for another 2 minutes then remove from heat and let it cool completely.

For leyali lebnan, in a large heavy saucepan, add the milk, semolina, sugar and cornstarch and whisk until fully combined. Bring the mixture to a simmer over medium-low heat until it starts to thicken, around 5 to 7 minutes. Make sure you continuously whisk to prevent the cream from burning. Now add the orange blossom water or rose water and mix gently to incorporate. Remove mixture from the stove and set aside.

Line a 9-inch (22-cm) cheesecake pan with parchment paper. Pour the mixture into the pan and let it cool for at least 10 minutes. Once it's cooled then cover it with plastic wrap and place it in the fridge for at least 5 to 6 hours for it to completely set. Once it has fully set, take it out of the fridge and add a layer of qishta and pistachios. Place it back in the fridge until you are ready to serve. Take it out of the pan, slice like a cake and pour sugar syrup just before serving. or you can leave that up to your guests. Serve a small jug of sugar syrup with a piece of layali lebnan.

Note *The original recipe calls for mastic beads to be added to the semolina layer. Since it's quite hard to find, I have chosen to omit it and replace it instead with cornstarch. However, if you would like to try it with mastic then grind 2 to 3 mastic pearls with 1 teaspoon of granulated sugar in a mortar, then add it to the semolina mixture instead of cornstarch.*

Tunisian Sabayon

Tunisian sabayon is custard-based pudding that is served chilled. It is not the same as Italian sabayon version as it doesn't have alcohol in it, but oil is used instead. It is flavored with fragrant orange blossom water and served cold. It has a pistachio or almond garnish and is often accompanied by fresh fruits and sometimes other pastries like bouscoutou *(a kind of sponge cake) or semolina cake.*

Yield 5 Servings

For the Pudding

10 large egg yolks

½ cup (100 g) granulated sugar

⅔ cup (160 ml) vegetable oil

1 tsp vanilla extract

2 tbsp (30 ml) orange blossom water

5 egg whites

For Garnishing

2–3 plums or peaches, sliced

In a stand mixer, with a whisk attachment, add the egg yolks and sugar and whisk on low speed. Pour in the oil gradually to create an emulsion. Mix it for about 6 to 8 minutes. Add in the vanilla extract and orange blossom water and mix for another 2 minutes. In a separate bowl, whisk the egg whites until peaks are formed, around 6 to 8 minutes. Fold the egg whites gently into the egg yolk mixture and mix until fully combined.

Pour the mixture gently into a loaf pan, cover with plastic wrap and freeze for at least 4 hours for up to 2 days. When it's ready, scoop with an ice cream scoop into fancy clear cups and garnish with slices of fruit.

Notes

- *Tunisian Sabayon can be eaten cold or melted.*
- *You can choose to omit the egg whites and not add it to the mixture, but it provides the pudding with a foamy and airy texture. Either way, it is still good without it.*

Sahlab

Sahlab, also known as sahlep and sahleb, is a delightful Middle Eastern pudding that has always been welcomed on a cold rainy day. It can also be made into a drink by using less cornstarch. Growing up in the U.K., the weather was mostly cold, and many months were filled with heavy snow. So, when we would come back home from playing in the snow, we had that warm bowl of sahlab ready for us. It was the highlight at the end of an amazing fun day making snowmen with carrot noses and large buttons for eyes. It can be served warm or cold and is sprinkled with some crushed pistachios and a hint of cinnamon on top. Although you can buy a ready-mix box of sahlab at any Middle Eastern store, it can never ever beat a homemade one.

Yield 6–8 Servings

For the Pudding

2 cups (480 ml) heavy cream

2 cups (480 ml) whole milk

¾ cup (150 g) granulated sugar

2 tbsp (30 g) cornstarch

1 tsp rose water or vanilla extract

⅓ cup (40 g) raisins (optional)

¼ cup (25 g) sweetened shredded coconut (optional)

For Garnishing

¼ cup (30 g) raw pistachio, crushed

Ground cinnamon

In a medium saucepan, add the cream and milk over medium heat. Next, add the sugar and cornstarch and whisk until fully combined. The mixture will start to thicken, around 5 to 7 minutes. Once it is thick, turn down the heat to low and add the rose water (or vanilla). Also add the raisins and coconut if you want to use them. Stir for another 2 minutes then remove from heat and pour into 6 to 8 serving bowls.

Garnish with a heap of pistachios and a sprinkle of cinnamon. You can serve it hot or cold. If you prefer it cold, place in the refrigerator for at least 1 hour and if not serve right away.

Roz Bi Haleeb

Rice pudding also known as roz bi haleeb *or* roz bi laban *can be found in so many cuisines including the Middle East. It is believed that rice pudding originated from the Middle East in medical texts rather than a recipe in a cookbook as it was usually recommended for people with an upset stomach. It's a very simple pudding consisting of rice, milk, sugar and cornstarch with rose water and/or orange blossom water for extra flavor. It is cooked over medium heat until it forms into a thick custard pudding perfect for warm weather. There are a lot of variations when it comes to rice pudding. It can also be served cold. Many different garnishes can be added like saffron, pistachios (or other crushed nuts), cinnamon, cream or honey. You can even serve it with a scoop of ice cream on top to give it more depth to the flavor profile.*

Yield 4–6 Servings

For the Pudding

4 cups (960 ml) whole milk, divided

2 cups (480 ml) half and half

1 cinnamon stick

1 cup (200 g) long grain white rice

¼ cup (50 g) granulated sugar

⅓ cup (50 g) cornstarch

1 tsp rose water

1 tbsp (15 ml) orange blossom water

For Garnishing

3-4 tbsp (21-30 g) crushed pistachios or a handful of pomegranate seeds

Rose petals (optional)

In a medium saucepot, add milk (reserve ¼ cup [60 ml]), half and half and cinnamon and let it boil over medium heat for 2 minutes. As soon as it starts to foam, remove the pot from the stove. Add the rice and sugar and mix well. (Do not wash the rice). Then, let it simmer for 20 minutes or until the rice is fully cooked.

When the rice is almost cooked, in a small bowl, mix the cornstarch with the reserved ¼ cup (60 ml) of milk and pour it into the pot. Next, add the rose water and orange blossom water and mix well. Continue to simmer. At this point it will start to thicken and have a creamier texture (around 5 minutes more). Remove the pudding from the heat and dispose of the cinnamon stick. Transfer the pudding to four large or six small bowls. Garnish with crushed pistachios and a dash of rose petals (if using).

Notes

- *Not washing the rice makes the pudding creamier as the starches in the rice are not washed away.*
- *Roz bi haleeb can be eaten as a dessert or for breakfast.*
- *You can add an additional ½ cup (100 g) of rice for a thicker consistency.*

Aish El Saraya

Aish el saraya is famously known as Lebanese bread pudding. It is made with toasted bread that is soaked in a caramel like syrup then topped off with a delicious layer of cream custard and crushed pistachios. This recipe is a delectable dessert that is eaten on special occasions. It does not contain eggs and is flavored with rose water and orange blossom water. It makes for a perfect dessert after any meal.

Yield 8 Servings

For the Pudding

1 (22-oz [625-g]) loaf of brioche bread (or white bread)

2 cups (400 g) granulated sugar

2 tbsp (30 g) unsalted butter

1 cup (240 ml) water, warm 130°F (55°C)

1 tsp vanilla extract (optional)

For the Cream Layer

2 cups (480 ml) whole milk

½ cup (60 g) cornstarch

2 cups (480 ml) heavy cream

⅓ cup (65 g) granulated sugar (optional)

1 tsp rose water

1 tsp orange blossom water

For Garnishing

½ cup (60 g) raw pistachios, crushed

Preheat oven to 350°F (180°C).

Place all the bread pieces on a baking sheet and bake for 5 to 7 minutes or until fully crispy and golden and toasted on both sides. (A typical loaf of brioche bread should have about 15 pieces). Take them out and let them cool completely. Once cooled, place the bread in a food processor and pulse 3 to 5 times until it breaks down into medium-sized pieces. Place the bread chunks in a bowl and set aside.

Next, add the sugar to a medium-sized saucepan over medium-low heat. Do not stir it until it starts melting, around 4 to 5 minutes. Once the sugar is completely melted, add the butter and whisk well until fully combined. Then add warm water gradually while whisking vigorously. Do not add it all at once. The process is very similar to making bechamel when adding milk slowly to avoid lumps. It will start becoming very bubbly and the sugar might harden slightly; however, just continue whisking until it starts melting again. Remove the pan from the heat and add vanilla and the bread pieces. Mix them together until fully combined. Prepare a 10-inch (25-cm) cheesecake pan by adding parchment paper all around the sides and the bottom. Slide in the soaked bread mixture and flatten evenly with a spatula. Let it cool for 10 minutes.

Prepare the cream layer by adding the milk and cornstarch to a saucepan over medium heat. Whisk until the cornstarch has completely dissolved to avoid lumps. Then add the cream and sugar (if you are using) and let the mixture thicken for about 7 minutes. Once it has thickened, remove the pan from the heat. Here you will add the rose water and the orange blossom water. Let it cool for 5 minutes then pour it on top of the bread layer. Once it has cooled down for at least 10 minutes, garnish with a layer of pistachios, then cover it with plastic wrap and cool in the fridge for at least 6 hours.

Note *You can add cream cheese or mascarpone instead of heavy cream.*

Ice Creams

If you've been to Middle Eastern and North African countries, then you know it can get pretty hot over there. Most months are hot with few months of moderately cold weather–depending on the country of course. Hence, ice cream plays a huge role in enduring those long, arduous months of scalding hot temperatures. Ice cream flavors use local and popular ingredients like pistachios, dates, date molasses, tahini and honey. My very first ice cream that I tasted back in Iraq was pistachio ice cream that was loaded with chunks of pistachios, bought from a famous ice cream store called Al Faqma. In the Al Karada area, where the lines were endless, everyone wanted to taste their famous pistachio ice cream. If you ask me now–was it worth it? I will tell you–100 percent. I have not been able to find anything remotely close to its taste, and that's why I had to find a way to make it at home.

Simple Booza

Arabic ice cream or booza, is a kind of ice cream with a consistency like mozzarella cheese. Booza's origin dates to at least 1500 AD in Greater Syria and is sometimes referred to as the "first ice cream in the world". It is elastic, sticky and resistant to melting in the hotter climates. The two main ingredients that give booza its unique taste and elasticity are mastic gum and sahlep (also called sahlab). Sahlep is a thickening agent made from dried orchid root. Be sure to buy only 100 percent pure sahlep as there are store bought ones with additives like sugar, cornstarch and added flavors. These will not give you the best results. The process of making this ice cream includes alternating freezing, stretching and pounding the ingredients. I know it might sound time consuming, but the result is very well worth it.

Yield 10–12 Servings

3-4 mastic granules

1½ cups (300 g) granulated sugar, divided

2 cups (480 ml) whole milk

2 cups (480 ml) heavy cream

2 tbsp (30 g) sahlep

1¾ cups (225 g) raw pistachios, finely crushed

With a mortar and pestle, grind the mastic granules with 1 teaspoon of sugar and set aside. In a heavy saucepan, add milk, cream, mastic mixture, sugar and sahlep. Simmer until the mixture starts to thicken, around 5 to 7 minutes. Remove the pan from the heat and let it completely cool down for 30 minutes. Add the mixture to a stand mixer and using the whisk attachment, whisk on low to medium speed for 2 to 3 minutes. Then place the bowl in the freezer for 1 hour, take it out and whisk again for 2 to 3 minutes, then place it back in the freezer for 2 hours.

Wrap a baking sheet entirely with a plastic wrap and cover with a layer of the pistachios. Take the ice cream out of the freezer and spread it on top of the pistachios. Make sure it covers all the pistachios. If the ice cream is a bit too hard to spread, let it rest for 5 minutes to slightly melt. Cover the baking sheet with plastic wrap and place it in the freezer for 1 hour. After 1 hour, take the ice cream out and remove the top plastic wrap. Take one end of the ice cream and using the bottom plastic wrap, start rolling it on to itself into a log shape. As you push the roll forward, pull the plastic wrap back and away so it doesn't get stuck in the ice cream. (This is similar to making Swiss rolls). When you have a completely rolled log, cover it with plastic wrap and roll it around to ensure the shape is perfectly round. Then, freeze for 5 to 6 hours. When you are ready to serve, slice it into circular pieces and serve immediately.

Note *Sahlep is a main ingredient in Arabic ice cream however due to its high price tag and its scarcity, it can be replaced with 4-5 tablespoons (32-40 g) of cornstarch. Although the texture will be slightly different as cornstarch tends to make it harder, whereas sahlep tends to make it stretchier. The only difference when it comes to preparation is that cornstarch needs to dissolve first in cold milk before it can be added to the rest of the ingredients to avoid lumps from forming. You also do not need to keep returning the mixture into the freezer, as it will instantly hold its shape when cold.*

No–Churn Halwa and Dibis Booza

Halwa is a Middle Eastern dessert made from sesame seed paste and sugar. Dibis is simply date paste. When you combine these unique flavors, you create something magical. I really cannot explain the taste in words as it's like nothing I have ever tasted before. But the best explanation I could give is it's nutty and sweet in taste and smooth with a velvety texture. Adding all those textures and flavors to the ice cream elevates it entirely and creates a new and improved way of enjoying ice cream in a Middle Eastern way. This recipe has very basic ingredients and is super easy to make.

Yield 4 Servings

2 cups (480 ml) heavy cream

1 tbsp (15 g) sahlep (optional)

1 (14-oz [396-g]) can sweetened condensed milk

½ cup (120 ml) tahini paste

½ cup (80 g) date paste

½ cup (60 g) raw pistachios, crushed

½ cup (65 g) halwa (optional)

In a stand mixer bowl, add the cream and whisk on medium speed until firm peaks start to form, around 5 to 7 minutes. Add the sahlep (if using) and mix for another 20 seconds. In a separate bowl, add the condensed milk and tahini and mix until well combined. Fold in the tahini mixture to the whipped cream until well combined. Pour the final mixture into a loaf pan. Add the date paste on top and using a knife, swirl the paste all around, giving it a swirled appearance. Place it in the freezer for 5 to 24 hours. Once it has set, take it out of the freezer and let it sit for 5 minutes before serving with a sprinkle of crushed pistachios and halwa threads.

Note *Sahlep is a main ingredient in Arabic ice creams however, due to its high price tag and its scarcity, it can be replaced with 2 to 3 tablespoons (16 to 24 g) of cornstarch, gradually added to the tahini mixture.*

Pistachio Booza

Pistachios have been consumed in the Middle East for thousands of years and have been used heavily in many of their desserts. When it comes to ice cream, pistachio is my go-to ice cream. The nuttiness of the pistachios, especially if they are slightly salty, makes it a favorite in my book.

Yield 6 Servings

2¼ cups (280 g) raw pistachio, crushed and divided

1 cup (200 g) granulated sugar, divided

5 large egg yolks

1 cup (240 ml) whole milk

2 cups (480 ml) heavy cream

Pinch of salt

1 tsp vanilla extract

Honey, for garnish

Add 1 cup (125 g) of the pistachios and ¼ cup (50 g) of the sugar to a food processor. Pulse on high speed until it becomes a bread-crumb-like consistency, around 3 to 5 minutes and then set aside. In a stand mixer bowl, add the egg yolks and the remaining sugar and beat until fluffy and the color is bright yellow, then set aside. In a medium saucepan, add milk, cream and salt over medium-low heat, until it reaches 180°F (80°C). Cook for 4 minutes stirring occasionally then remove from heat. Add a small amount of the heated milk mixture to the egg yolks while whisking constantly for 1 minute. Then pour the egg mixture back into the pot of milk mixture and stir constantly over low heat until it starts to form a thick custard consistency, about 4 to 6 minutes. Remove from the heat and add the vanilla and pistachio paste. For garnishing, add 2 to 4 table-spoons of honey (optional). Whisk well until the sugar has been fully dissolved.

Pour the mixture in a loaf pan, cover with plastic wrap and refrigerate for 3 to 4 hours or overnight. Freeze an ice cream bowl overnight as well. Once completely chilled, add the mixture to the bowl of your ice cream maker and follow instructions of the manufacturer. Next, add the remaining pistachios into the mixture. Scoop from the ice cream bowl and add to a freeze-safe container and place in the freezer. Take it out when ready to serve, scoop in serving bowls, sprinkle more pistachios and serve with a drizzle of honey.

Note *If the ice cream seems to be a bit chunky, you can blend it with an immersion blender then place it back in the container and freeze.*

Booza Ala Tamur

I didn't grow up eating dates for the first ten years of my life, just because it wasn't that popular or easy to attain in the U.K. However, once we got back to the Middle East, it was everywhere. I remember going back home to Baghdad and from the airport I would see hundreds and thousands of palm trees in the fields along the way. The sun was beaming down hard on them, which created such majestic shadows on the ground that I cannot put into words—but I remember them so vividly. I was honestly shocked by how many palm trees can exist in one place. Little did I know that every single house in Baghdad had one or two—at the minimum and those trees would produce an insanely large number of dates. They would start from the hard, starchy yellow skin and continue to ripen into half brown and yellow, (which a lot of people loved to eat at this stage), then continues to ripen fully to the brown color that we are all familiar with. We would add it to most of our desserts, drinks or even enjoy by itself. One of the things I loved eating later on was a combination of softened dates with ice cream and enjoying it during those long months of hot weather. It was naturally sweetened without adding any sugar and would produce a slight caramel-like taste when combined with the ice cream, making it one of my favorite things to eat.

Yield 4 Servings

For the Ice Cream

1 tsp sahlep or ⅓ cup (40 g) cornstarch

1½ cups (360 ml) whole milk, cold, divided

1½ cups (360 ml) heavy cream

1 tsp cardamom

Pinch of salt

1½ cups (360 g) medjool dates, pitted and divided

1 cup (240 ml) sour cream

For Garnishing

⅔ cup (75 g) raw pistachios, crushed

2-3 tbsp (30-45 ml) date syrup

Freeze your ice cream maker bowl the night before making it. In a different bowl, mix the sahlep or cornstarch with ½ cup (120 ml) of the milk and set aside. In a saucepan, add the remainder of the milk, cream, cardamom and salt. Place the pan over medium-high heat and let it come to a boil, then pour in the starch mixture. Turn down the heat to medium-low while whisking until it thickens. Once it has thickened, remove from the heat and set aside.

In a food processor, add 1 cup (240 g) of the dates and the sour cream and process until the dates start to combine well with the cream, around 2 minutes. Add half of the milk mixture and continue processing for 2 minutes. Then gradually add the remaining half and process until the mixture is smooth and creamy, around 2 to 3 minutes. Take the ice cream bowl out of the freezer and place the mixture in it. Roughly chop the remaining ½ cup (120 g) of the dates and add it to the ice cream mixture while mixing with a spatula until well combined. Place it in the freezer overnight.

Once it is fully frozen, take it out and let it rest for 5 minutes. To serve, take a large scoop and place the ice cream in a serving bowl, sprinkle with crushed pistachios and a drizzle of date syrup.

Hot Beverages

Tea in Arabic is known as *chai*. It is more commonly consumed than coffee throughout the Arabian culture to this day. Offering tea is an integral part of Arab hospitality and business etiquette. It is served to guests as a welcoming drink. It is considered rude to reject that welcoming tea when offered. Tea is usually made into a strong, dark and sugared tea, like the Arabic black tea also known as Chai Aswad (page 165). It is served in clear glass cups called *istikan* that come with a saucer or in tall colored glasses for the mint tea. Another popular type of tea is cardamom tea which is my absolute favorite. Arabs like to consume tea at every meal and directly after the meal. There is also a teatime between lunch and dinner where tea is served with Arabic sweets and biscuits. Growing up with my family, I used to oversee the teatime and prepare all of those small, bite-sized sweets, along with some well brewed black tea. When it comes to choosing the right kind of tea, loose leaf is the best and tea bags are not recommended if you want to achieve the authentic taste. When it comes to coffee, which in Arabic is Qahwa (page 169); it is not consumed quite as much as tea and is mainly served for special celebrations. The most common qahwa in the Middle East is the "Arabic qahwa" that is sort of similar to Turkish coffee but has its own unique taste profile. In this chapter, I will share some of the most popular ones that I grew up drinking and to this day, enjoy drinking daily.

Chai Aswad

Back in my mum's kitchen, she had this small green kerosene portable heater that came with three heating cores and three knobs that you would turn clockwise or counterclockwise to increase or decrease the heat. She would specifically use that portable heater to brew the tea pot. It wouldn't matter when you wanted your cup of tea, there always would be a pot there lightly brewing on the heater and replaced with a fresh new pot when it was empty. There is a lot of culture and etiquette on how to serve black tea, when to serve it and to whom you are serving it. When it came to my family, they would either use istikan, *which is a long thin type of glass that comes with its own saucer, or just a regular cup. Sugar cubes were either presented in the saucer beside the istikan or added directly inside of it and it was served at the end of a meal with a "preferable" piece of dessert.*

Yield 2 Cups (480 ml)

2 cups (480 ml) water

3 black tea bags or 3 tbsp (6 g) Ceylon loose-leaf tea

2 cardamom pods, broken

1 pinch saffron thread (optional)

In a tea pot, add the water and bring to a boil over medium heat. Next, add the tea, cardamom and saffron (if you are using) then cover the pot with its lid and lower the heat to the lowest temperature possible. Let it slightly brew for 5 minutes. The more it brews, the darker and stronger it will be. Strain into a cup if you are using the loose black tea leaves and sweeten with sugar if desired.

Notes

- *Presentation is key if you are planning on serving it Arabian style. The pot should be arranged on a serving tray surrounded by small tea glasses or cups. Large cups or mugs are uncommon. Allow guests to serve themselves from a sugar bowl to accommodate different tastes and preferences.*

- *There are many varieties and brands when buying black tea. I would suggest regular black tea or even better is the Ceylon black tea from brands like Ahmad Tea®, Alwazah Tea®, PG Tips®, Twinings® and Tetley®. If those are not available, you can go with Earl Grey or English Breakfast. The taste might be slightly different, but these are the closest to regular black tea.*

Chai Bi Heil

For as long as I can remember, I have been drinking cardamom tea at least 3 to 4 times a day. There is something simply irresistible that comes from that slight hint of cardamom in brewed black tea. Chai bi heil is quite a traditional herbal tea that is heavily consumed in the Middle Eastern cuisine. It is made by infusing a few cardamom seeds or full pods in a pot of black tea that is being brewed. It can be drunk with or without sugar and milk, but my preference is with both as I have found the combination of cardamom and milk to be delicious. I am drinking one right now while I'm typing this—I cannot get enough! There are a few variations of making cardamom tea like adding honey, ginger, cinnamon sticks and/or cloves to it, however my method is simply 2 ingredients—black loose-leaf tea and cardamom pods. When it comes to brewing time, it really depends on the type of tea, brand and your preference. Brewing for too long will make your tea taste very bitter and if you don't brew it long enough, the tea will have little flavor with no body.

Yield 4 Cups (960 ml)

4 cups (960 ml) water

1 tbsp (2 g) black loose-leaf tea

2 green cardamom pods, cracked

1 tsp honey (optional)

In a pot, add water and bring to a boil over high heat. Next, add the loose tea leaves and cardamom pods directly to the boiling water or in a tea infuser and place it inside the water. Cover, reduce the heat to low and let it brew gently for 5 minutes. Remove the tea infuser or pour into a tea strainer and into a glass teacup. Serve while hot.

Note *You can use ground cardamom instead of cardamom pods. Replace every cardamom pod with ½ teaspoon of ground cardamom.*

Chai Bi Ni'Naa

Also known as Moroccan mint tea, this tea is traditionally consumed in Morocco, Tunisia, Algeria and a few other Middle Eastern countries. It is a green tea that is infused with spearmint leaves and is generally very sweet. The main ingredients are green tea, fresh mint leaves, sugar and boiling water. It is made by steeping green tea with a generous amount of spearmint leaves and is traditionally served in small glass cups. You might even find another variation of adding pine seeds to give it a nutty flavor and you can chew on them while drinking the mint tea. My favorite thing about mint tea, apart from the delicious taste, is how it is presented and poured. The person pouring the tea usually pours it at an arm length height as a sign of hospitality—the higher the tea is poured—the more welcome the guests are. It also helps to create the desirable foamy head that occurs on the top of the tea when this is done. This wonderful tea can be served by itself or with some desserts and pastries.

Yield 6 Cups (1.4 L)

1 bunch spearmint, fresh

6 cups (1.4 L) water

3 tbsp (6 g) green loose-leaf tea

¼ cup (50 g) granulated sugar

Handful of pine nuts, toasted

Start by removing the mint stems, washing the leaves and then patting them dry. Add water to a pot and bring to a boil, then reduce the heat and add the tea leaves, mint leaves and the sugar. Turn the heat down to low and steep for 5 minutes. Add 1 to 2 teaspoons (2 to 4 g) of pine nuts to each serving glass before pouring in the tea. Once the tea is steeped, remove from heat and serve. To froth the tea, pour into the glasses from a height. Serve while hot and preferably with a dessert.

Notes

- *If you do not like the bitterness of the tea, you can first wash the tea in 1 cup (240 ml) of boiling water by swirling it in the pot for 30 seconds then straining the leaves out and disposing the water. This process helps in reducing some of the tannins that give the tea its harsh and bitter flavor. After washing the tea leaves, add them back into the pot with the sugar, mint leaves and the boiling water and slightly simmer for 5 minutes.*

- *While gunpowder tea or loose-leaf green tea provides you with the best result for this kind of tea, you can also use regular black tea leaves in a 1:1 ratio. Honey is also used as a substitute for sugar so add it along with the tea leaves.*

- *Mint tea can also be consumed as cold tea. Simply place it in the fridge after brewing for at least 2 hours. You can also add ice cubes to it for a better, more refreshing experience.*

- *One small sprig of mint can be added to each glass along with the pine nuts before pouring the tea in the glasses. It gives it a more intense flavor, and some people like to add the mint leaves only after the tea has been steeped to give it a fresher and lighter taste.*

Karak Chai

Karak chai is a strong tea in both taste and color compared to a regular black tea. It is made by brewing black tea leaves with evaporated milk and a mixture of aromatic spices and herbs like black pepper, cardamom, cinnamon, fennel and cloves. It is sweet in flavor with a caramel color. It originated from India and grew very popular in the Arabian Gulf region. I remember my first time trying it in Dubai and it took me by surprise. Although I consider myself a tea connoisseur, chai karak still took me by surprise. It was my first time drinking spiced tea and I was truly impressed. There is such a unique balance of flavor between all the ingredients that makes it the perfect cup of tea in the cold wintertime or any time really. A lot of people might confuse it with chai masala, but they are quite different as karak will only have two to three spices whereas chai masala has a much longer list of spices like cinnamon, peppercorns, star anise and many more.

Yield 3 Cups (720 ml)

2 tbsp (30 g) granulated sugar

2 cups (480 ml) hot water

1 tbsp (2 g) high quality black loose-leaf tea

2 green cardamom pods, crushed

½-inch (1.25-cm) cinnamon stick

1 whole clove

Pinch of saffron threads (2–3 threads)

1 slice of whole ginger root (optional)

¼ cup (30 ml) evaporated milk

In a medium saucepan over medium heat, add the sugar and let it melt without stirring it until it caramelizes and becomes golden. Slowly add the hot water, do not worry if some pieces of the sugar harden, it will melt in the end. Next, add the tea leaves, cardamom pods, cinnamon, clove, saffron and ginger (if you are using). Let it boil for 7 minutes on medium-low heat. After the time is up, add the evaporated milk and let it boil for 2 minutes, then lower the heat to low. Cover the pot and let it simmer for 8 minutes until you notice the tea to be a bit thicker. Transfer to a tea pot and using a tea strainer, pour into teacups and serve while hot.

Notes

- *If you are not a big fan of spices, then you can reduce them to your liking.*

- *Leftover karak can be stored in the refrigerator for 2 to 3 days and can be reheated in the microwave or over the stove before serving.*

Qahwa

Qahwa or kahwa *is made from roasted coffee beans and cardamom (and sometimes saffron), which gives it that unique, delicious, robust and slightly bitter taste. It is preferably served with dates, dried figs or any other sweet to counteract the bitter taste. It has been an integral part of Arab culture and Arabic hospitality for centuries and its preparation and serving are linked to elaborate traditions and rituals. Traditionally, qahwa is served for special celebrations like a wedding, a child's birth, upon a guest's arrival and on certain holidays. If you have ever visited the Arab region, more specifically the Arabian Peninsula, then you may have witnessed a coffee ceremony where the host conducts the whole process of roasting, grinding, brewing and serving the coffee right in front of their guests. It is brewed in a* dallah *(a traditional Arabic coffee pot) for about 20 minutes then carefully transferred to another dallah that is made specifically to pour into the small serving cups without handles called* finjan. *It is fine if you do not own a dallah, as you can prepare qahwa in a pot on the stove.*

One of the most loveable things about qahwa is the act of reading *a finjan—or fortune telling which is an art in itself. To begin reading, you drink your coffee, then flip the finjan upside down on the saucer, facing towards you, using your right hand. Then the finjan must rest there for 5 minutes to help the lines form and dry out a bit. The reader will then proceed to read those lines to "predict your future." Although it is superstitious at best, the whole experience is very enjoyable and entertaining. I remember my sister was a really good reader and we would wait for our turn for her to read our finjan after drinking the qahwa. She always had a way of interpreting patterns, letters and words that I couldn't see even if I squinted so hard and racked my brain; I just couldn't see it! It is a talent that I, unfortunately, didn't have or couldn't learn but nonetheless was able to enjoy being on the receiving end of it.*

Yield 2 Cups (480 ml)

2 tbsp (16 g) Arabica roasted coffee beans, finely ground

½ tbsp (3 g) ground cardamom

2 cups (480 ml) water

Sugar or honey (optional)

In a bowl combine both the coffee and cardamom and mix well. Using either a dallah or a small saucepan, bring the water to a boil over medium heat. Add the coffee mixture and reduce heat to low and let it brew for 8 to 10 minutes. You will notice a foam that will rise to the top so you will need to remove the pot from the heat to prevent it from overflowing and potentially losing that foam. The foam is considered one of the most essential parts of coffee and coffee is not the same without it.

After 8 to 10 minutes, remove the coffee from the stove and let it rest for 2 minutes to allow the coffee granules to settle at the bottom of the pot. Serve in small cups, add sugar or honey to your liking and enjoy while hot.

Acknowledgments

To my mum: Thank you for "patiently" teaching me the true essence of cooking at such an early age. Thank you for sparking and igniting the passion that has led me to where I am today. Thank you for always picking up the phone and teaching me recipes that I never knew existed in our culture. I wouldn't be where I am today, so thank you Mammy. I hope this book makes you proud.

To my dad: Thank you for the continuous stories about our family history that you so passionately talk about all the time; it eventually helped me to better understand my roots and where I came from. It also helped me understand what I want to present and teach through my cooking and how to preserve all our food through writing and sharing. You also taught me how to be a better storyteller and to put all my heart into everything I write, so thank you, Baba.

To my husband "Mothana," my one true love and soulmate: Where do I even begin to thank you for all that you have done for me throughout the past 20 years, I owe EVERY-THING to you. I am what I am because of your support, your patience, your love, your guidance and your constant encouragement and those confidence-boosting pep talks that you always provide so freely and effortlessly every time I am down, and for providing me with your "out of the box" ideas that have helped me shape and re-define my career and overall approach to food and business. Thank you for giving me my space and for helping me spread my wings so I can learn what and who I really want to be. I could not have asked for a better partner than you, you are my blessing now and forever, therefore, I dedicate this book in its entirety to you hbibi!

To Naya & Adam: My babies and the joy to my life, if it wasn't for the love you have for my food and your pure excitement in always trying something new, I wouldn't have had the encouragement I needed to further explore my heritage through food and discover the wonderful recipes it holds. Thank you for your honesty in telling me how my food really tasted like even when you didn't like it that much. Because of that, I learned how to improve them and make them even better. Thank you for your unconditional love that helped shape me into the mom I am today. I hope this book will be your gateway to learn more about our culture and food and "hopefully" not having to call me all the time asking me how to prepare a certain Arabic dessert when you're older. It's all in here, my loves.

To my sister and partner in crime "Jena": I could never imagine a life without you, and growing up with you has been the highlight of my childhood years as it has shaped the very bond we have today. I cherish our sisterhood and the friendship we have, and I love how strong it has become and that nothing has ever been able to come between us all these years and I know for a fact that nothing will. You have all my heart and forever love, thank you for being the best big sister I could ever hope for, and making me an aunt to my favorite nephews, Yousif and Yasir . . . you are my rock Chanchoon.

To my in-laws: Thank you Amo for encouraging me years and years ago to write my cookbook and to take it more seriously. I'll never forget how enthusiastically you would tell me "Write one recipe every day and in no time, you will have a complete cookbook, it's that easy if you put your mind to it." I also wouldn't have considered starting my own business if it wasn't for you planting the idea to sell my creations after tasting them and loving them so much. I owe you a lot for creating that "business mentality" inside of me. It started there and then and has never stopped. To Khala, thank you for your outpouring and unconditional love you have given me throughout all these years, I am forever grateful.

To my friends: Thank you for always being there for me, pushing me and encouraging me every single step of the way, I would have had the hardest of times without those encouragement texts and chats.

To Sondra: Thank you for being the best neighbor and taste tester I could have ever hoped for. Thank you for always encouraging me and getting excited every time I bring you a new dish to try. Your feedback and words of encouragement have always been the highlight of that day. I am fortunate to call you my neighbor and friend.

To Page Street Publishing Company: Thank you for believing in me and giving me this opportunity to write my very first cookbook. I have dreamt of this for the last 10 years and it's now not a dream anymore but a reality—all because of you.

To Kara Chin: Thank you for bringing my vision of each and every single dish that I had inside my head into reality. I could not have asked for a better photographer for my very first cookbook.

To you: Last but not least, to you, reading this now. Thank you for believing in me and buying my first cookbook. I'm so humbled by your love and support whether just now or that you have been with me throughout my cooking journey throughout the last 12 years. This book has been a tremendous labor of love, and for you to notice that and buy it, I can never thank you enough. I truly hope you enjoy it and try a dessert or two or even more, from this book.

About the Author

Lamees AttarBashi is an MBA engineer turned award-winning chef and TV host. She is an international culinary enthusiast with a focus on Arabian cuisine, a recipe developer, constant nomad and now an immigrant. She spent most of her years traveling the world and learning about different cuisines and food. Her passion for food led her to pursue a diploma in Hot Kitchen from ICCA (International Center for Culinary Arts) in Dubai which is accredited by City & Guilds UK and recognized by the World Association of Chefs' Societies and the Government of Dubai, UAE. She holds various certificates of cooking with many international and Michelin star chefs. As a result, Lamees gained notice from major TV channels in Dubai and was offered a TV show under her name "Lamees's Dining Table" where she got to showcase her love for Arabian and international food to her fans and followers along with regular appearances on popular TV shows and food festivals. Lamees is on a mission to showcase Arabian food in a fun and approachable way. She truly believes that food is a universal language and is a way to connect with other people, hoping that her recipes will be like a gateway into this untapped cuisine. She is currently in the process of launching two bootstrapped CPG startups in 2024.

Index

A

Aish El Saraya, 153

almonds

Almond Briouat, 91–92

Almond Cake, 49

Namoura, 39–40

Umm Ali, 141

anise seeds (yansoon)

Kaak Al Asawir, 73–74

Maamoul, 68

Maarouk, 24–26

Asawir Il Sit, 96–98

B

Baghrir Cake with Rose Infused Frosting, 50

Baid Al Qata, 85

Baklawa Bites, 109

Baklawa Cheesecake, 58

Baklawa Pull Apart Bread, 20

Balah Al Sham, 125

Barazek, 71–72

beverages

Chai Aswad, 165

Chai Bi Heil, 166

Chai Bi Ni'Naa, 167

Karak Chai, 168

Qahwa, 169

biscuits and cookies

Baid Al Qata, 85

Barazek, 71–72

Coconut Cookies, 77

Date Balls, 82

Ghuraibah, 78

Kaak Al Asawir, 73–74

Kleicha, 67

Maamoul, 68

Simsimiya, 81

Booza Ala Tamur, 162

breads

Baklawa Pull Apart Bread, 20

Cheese Manakeesh Flatbread, 19

Churak, 23

Kaak Youyou, 34

Khaliat Al Nahl, 33

Maarouk, 24–26

Pistachio Cardamom Rolls, 27–29

Simit, 30

Burma, 106

C

cakes and cheesecakes

Almond Cake, 49

Baghrir Cake with Rose Infused Frosting, 50

Baklawa Cheesecake, 58

Dates and Walnuts with Salted Caramel Cake, 45

Fig Jam Cold Cheesecake, 61

Khanfaroosh, 57

Kunafa Cheesecake, 41–42

Lazy Cake, 62

Namoura, 39–40

Pistachio Cake, 46

Qurs Akili Cake, 54

Sponge Cake with Pomegranate Glaze, 53

cardamom

Baid Al Qata, 85

Chai Aswad, 165

Chai Bi Heil, 166

Ghuraibah, 78

Karak Chai, 168

Khanfaroosh, 57

Kleicha, 67

Maamoul, 68

Maarouk, 24–26

My Mum's Baklawa, 89–90

Pistachio Cardamom Rolls, 27–29

Qahwa, 169

Qurs Akili Cake, 54

Umm Ali, 141

Chai Aswad, 165

Chai Bi Heil, 166

Chai Bi Ni'Naa, 167

Cheese Manakeesh Flatbread, 19

cheesecakes. See cakes and cheesecakes

chocolate

Lazy Cake, 62

Phyllo Cigars, 102

Churak, 23

coconut

Coconut Cookies, 77

Date Balls, 82

Namoura, 39–40

Sahlab, 149

cream cheese

Baklawa Cheesecake, 58

Fig Jam Cold Cheesecake, 61

Ishtaliah, 142

Khaliat Al Nahl, 33

Kunafa Cheesecake, 41–42

Pistachio Cake, 46

Rose Infused Frosting, 50

D

dates

Booza Ala Tamur, 162

Date Balls, 82

Dates and Walnuts with Salted Caramel Cake, 45

Kaak Al Asawir, 73–74

Kleicha, 67

Maamoul, 68

Maarouk, 24–26

No-Churn Halwa and Dibis Booza, 158

Simit, 30

F

fennel seeds

Kaak Al Asawir, 73–74

Maamoul, 68

feta cheese, in Cheese Manakeesh Flatbread, 19

Fig Jam Cold Cheesecake, 61

G

Ghuraibah, 78

glucose syrup

Balah Al Sham, 125

Zlabiya, 122

H

Halawat Il Jibn, 134–135

Halwa, 137

Halwa and Dibis Booza, 158

heavy cream

Aish El Saraya, 153

Baklawa Cheesecake, 58

Booza Ala Tamur, 162

Fig Jam Cold Cheesecake, 61

Ishtaliah, 142

Kunafa Cheesecake, 41–42

Kunafa Rolls, 117

No-Churn Halwa and Dibis Booza, 158

Pistachio Booza, 161

Qishta, 95, 99, 114, 126, 129, 134, 145

Rose Infused Frosting, 50

Rose Water Cream, 29

Sahlab, 149

Salted Caramel, 45

Simple Booza, 157

Umm Ali, 141

honey

Almond Briouat, 91–92

Almond Cake, 49

Baklawa Cheesecake, 58

Honey Syrup, 58, 129, 132

Khaliat Al Nahl, 33

Qatayif, 129–131

Simsimiya, 81

Stuffed Qatayif, 132

I

ice creams

Booza Ala Tamur, 162

No-Churn Halwa and Dibis Booza, 158

Pistachio Booza, 161

Simple Booza, 157

Ishtaliah, 142

K

Kaak Al Asawir, 73–74

Kaak Youyou, 34

Karak Chai, 168

kataifi dough

Kunafa, 113

Kunafa Rolls, 117

Osmalieh, 114

Khaliat Al Nahl, 33

Khanfaroosh, 57

Kleicha, 67

Kunafa, 113

Kunafa Cheesecake, 41–42

Kunafa Rolls, 117

L

Lazy Cake, 62

Leyali Lebnan, 145

Lukaimat, 121

M

Maamoul, 68

Maarouk, 24–26

Mafrouka, 126–128

mozzarella cheese

Cheese Manakeesh Flatbread, 19

Halawat Il Jibn, 134–135
Kunafa, 113
Kunafa Rolls, 117
Muakaja, 105
My Mum's Baklawa, 89–90

N

Namoura, 39–40
No-Churn Halwa and Dibis Booza, 158
Nutella
    Asawir Il Sit, 96–98
    Lukaimat, 121

O

orange blossom water
    Aish El Saraya, 153
    Halawat Il Jibn, 134–135
    Ishtaliah, 142
    Kaak Youyou, 34
    Leyali Lebnan, 145
    Osmalieh, 114
    Qishta, 95, 99
    Roz Bi Haleeb, 150
    Tunisian Sabayon, 146
    Umm Ali, 141
Osmalieh, 114

P

Phyllo Cigars, 102
phyllo dough
    Almond Briouat, 91–92
    Asawir Il Sit, 96–98
    Baklawa Bites, 109
    Baklawa Cheesecake, 58
    Burma, 106

Muakaja, 105
My Mum's Baklawa, 89–90
Phyllo Cigars, 102
Warbat Bil Qishta, 95
Zinood Il Sit, 99–101
pine nuts
    Date Balls, 82
    Umm Ali, 141
pistachios
    Aish El Saraya, 153
    Asawir Il Sit, 96–98
    Baklawa Bites, 109
    Baklawa Cheesecake, 58
    Baklawa Pull Apart Bread, 20
    Barazek, 71–72
    Burma, 106
    Date Balls, 82
    Fig Jam Cold Cheesecake, 61
    Ghuraibah, 78
    Halawat Il Jibn, 134–135
    Halwa, 137
    Kaak Youyou, 34
    Kunafa Rolls, 117
    Leyali Lebnan, 145
    Mafrouka, 126–128
    Muakaja, 105
    No-Churn Halwa and Dibis Booza, 158
    Osmalieh, 114
    Phyllo Cigars, 102
    Pistachio Booza, 161
    Pistachio Cake, 46
    Pistachio Cardamom Rolls, 27–29
    Qatayif, 129–131
    Roz Bi Haleeb, 150

Sahlab, 149
Simple Booza, 157
Umm Ali, 141
Warbat Bil Qishta, 95
Zinood Il Sit, 99–101
Pomegranate Glaze, 53
puddings
    Aish El Saraya, 153
    Ishtaliah, 142
    Leyali Lebnan, 145
    Roz Bi Haleeb, 150
    Sahlab, 149
    Tunisian Sabayon, 146
    Umm Ali, 141

Q

Qahwa, 169
Qatayif, 129–131
Qishta (ishta)
    Halawat Il Jibn, 134–135
    Leyali Lebnan, 145
    Mafrouka, 126–128
    Osmalieh, 114
    Qatayif, 129–131
    Warbat Bil Qishta, 95
    Zinood Il Sit, 99–101
Qurs Akili Cake, 54

R

raisins
    Sahlab, 149
    Umm Ali, 141
rice and rice flour
    Khanfaroosh, 57
    Roz Bi Haleeb, 150

Rose Infused Frosting, 50

rose water
Aish El Saraya, 153
Almond Briouat, 91–92
Balah Al Sham, 125
Ishtaliah, 142
Leyali Lebnan, 145
Pistachio Cake frosting, 46
Qishta, 95, 99
Rose Infused Frosting, 50
Rose Water Cream, 29
Roz Bi Haleeb, 150
Sahlab, 149
Roz Bi Haleeb, 150

S

saffron
Karak Chai, 168
Khanfaroosh, 57
Qurs Akili Cake, 54
Sahlab, 149
semolina
Baghrir Cake, 50
Halawat Il Jibn, 134–135
Kaak Al Asawir, 73–74
Leyali Lebnan, 145
Maamoul, 68
Mafrouka, 126-128
Namoura, 39–40
Qatayif, 129-131
sesame seeds
Almond Briouat, 91–92
Barazek, 71–72
Date Balls, 82

Kaak Al Asawir, 73–74
Qurs Akili Cake, 54
Simsimiya, 81
Simit, 30
Simple Booza, 157
Simple Sugar Syrup
about, 12
Asawir Il Sit, 96–98
Baklawa Bites, 109
Baklawa Pull Apart Bread, 20
Balah Al Sham, 125
Burma, 106
Halawat Il Jibn, 134–135
Kaak Youyou, 34
Kunafa, 113
Kunafa Cheesecake, 41–42
Kunafa Rolls, 117
Leyali Lebnan, 145
Lukaimat, 121
Muakaja, 105
My Mum's Baklawa, 89–90
Namoura, 39–40
Osmalieh, 114
Phyllo Cigars, 102
Warbat Bil Qishta, 95
Zinood Il Sit, 99–101
Simsimiya, 81
spearmint, in Chai Bi Ni'Naa, 167
Sponge Cake with Pomegranate Glaze, 53
Stuffed Qatayif, 132
sweetened condensed milk
Lazy Cake, 62
No-Churn Halwa and Dibis Booza, 158

T

tahini
Halwa, 137
No-Churn Halwa and Dibis Booza, 158
Qurs Akili Cake, 54
Tunisian Sabayon, 146

U

Umm Ali, 141

W

walnuts
Baid Al Qata, 85
Baklawa Bites, 109
Baklawa Pull Apart Bread, 20
Dates and Walnuts with Salted Caramel Cake, 45
My Mum's Baklawa, 89–90
Phyllo Cigars, 102
Stuffed Qatayif, 132
Warbat Bil Qishta, 95

Y

yogurt, Greek
Baklawa Cheesecake, 58
Namoura, 39–40
Pistachio Cake, 46

Z

Zinood Il Sit, 99–101
Zlabiya, 122